Your Life Was Never
Meant to be a Struggle

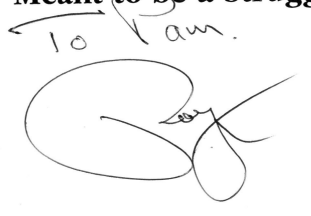

To Pam.

Roy E. Klienwachter

TRAFFORD
PUBLISHING™

Note for Librarians: A cataloguing record for this book is available from Library and Archives Canada at www.collectionscanada.ca/amicus/index-e.html
ISBN 1-4120-7752-4

Printed in Victoria, BC, Canada. Printed on paper with minimum 30% recycled fibre. Trafford's print shop runs on "green energy" from solar, wind and other environmentally-friendly power sources.

TRAFFORD
PUBLISHING™

Offices in Canada, USA, Ireland and UK
This book was published *on-demand* in cooperation with Trafford Publishing. On-demand publishing is a unique process and service of making a book available for retail sale to the public taking advantage of on-demand manufacturing and Internet marketing. On-demand publishing includes promotions, retail sales, manufacturing, order fulfilment, accounting and collecting royalties on behalf of the author.

Book sales for North America and international:
Trafford Publishing, 6E–2333 Government St.,
Victoria, BC V8T 4P4 CANADA
phone 250 383 6864 (toll-free 1 888 232 4444)
fax 250 383 6804; email to orders@trafford.com
Book sales in Europe:
Trafford Publishing (UK) Limited, 9 Park End Street, 2nd Floor
Oxford, UK OX1 1HH UNITED KINGDOM
phone 44 (0)1865 722 113 (local rate 0845 230 9601)
facsimile 44 (0)1865 722 868; info.uk@trafford.com
Order online at:
trafford.com/05-2648

10 9 8 7 6 5 4 3 2 1

YOUR LIFE WAS NEVER MEANT TO BE A STRUGGLE

ABOUT THE COVER

A native of Ontario Canada, I have made B.C. my home for close to two decades. What an inspiring place to live as an artist, with the scenery and nature all around me for inspiration. My work includes many media and subjects. I have no favourite as I enjoy variety. I am very experienced in the arts, so it seemed natural that I share with others, and I have enjoyed instructing for almost three decades. The painting on the cover is a sea stack. This particular one is on the west coast of Vancouver Island at Spring Island, Kuquot Sound. I have visited the west side of Vancouver Island several times. It has many such offerings for the artistic palette.

Judy Shield
www.myartclub.com/j.shield

2 YOUR LIFE WAS NEVER MEANT TO BE A STRUGGLE

For Vicky, with love and respect.
She came
to me a stranger
and said, "Roy, 'I am your Guardian Angel',"
and then stayed with me for the
next three years to see me through
a difficult time.

YOUR LIFE WAS NEVER MEANT TO BE A STRUGGLE
By Roy E. Klienwachter

"*YOUR LIFE WAS NEVER MEANT TO BE A STRUGGLE*," is for those who are ready to move to the next step in their awareness.

INTRODUCTION TO THIS BOOK

This book is about self empowerment and an awareness of the awesome power that you possess to create anything that you think about or desire.

The truth about whom, and what, you are has been kept from you for centuries, because those that would guide us believed that you were not mature enough to handle it. This may, or may not, be true. Even today there are many who would not be able to use it positively. Sudden power is destructive and in our history those that have achieved it have destroyed themselves, drunken on the awesome power with which they have access.

There is a huge assumption here by our teachers and guides that we are not ready for this information. When is the *right* time, and who are they to judge?

Why have we given them the powers to limit our power in the first place, are we really that immature even after centuries of compliance?

The decision to use this power has always remained with the individual ego—you. Each and every one of you has your finger on the button. The ability to push the button is regulated by fear. This fear is something you have learned to live with throughout your lives. It is something that you have learned from childhood. It is what you have known as true since childhood. You are not deserving and are less than that which created you. You have been warned not to go there less you be eternally damned.

Fear is a paper shackle that can be ripped open with a single thought.

With great power comes great responsibility, and possibly that is what humanity fears the most. With total responsibility comes great truth. In the physical realm, total honestly is not possible because you live within the greatest lie of all—that you exist. Life is an illusion, and it is the image of your thoughts that exists.

The lie of self is what has given you your individuality, and separated you from what you really are. It is what you have based all your physical awareness on. You perpetuate the lie even further with each waking moment that you are physically aware.

Awareness does not change that lie, it just means you can see through it. It means you now have access to the power that is naturally yours. It brings you back to the awareness that all is perfect the way it is. It also gives you opportunity to change it. To change all the circumstances of your own life, you become pro-active in it, instead of re-active.

The only purpose to life is to find life experience it, and create more life. It is a continuing process, not an end.

There is no purpose to our own lives accept for the purpose that we give it individually. That which created us is life, and so are we. We are the sum of its parts, and have all the attributes of that life force. We are eternally connected, and live in an illusion of time and space.

This book is the marriage of four ebooks that I have written over the past five years while studying my favourite subject of manifesting.

One book would have done it, and manifesting or creating something from nothing covers all other subjects. If one learns how to manifest effectively there would be no need to write a book on health or spirituality. Manifesting is something we do both on a conscious and subconscious level in every second of every hour of every day. We are all great manifestors, and for the most part that creation is done subconsciously.

It is said that opportunity only knocks once in a lifetime, which is incorrect; it happens continuously because we create the opportunities ourselves and then choose from them.

Should we learn how to create effectively, we would be able to manifest good health, abundance, joy, peace, and happiness consciously.

This book was created to tell you that it is possible with very little effort to create anything that you desire on a conscious level, and on demand.

The other books included in this publication are more of a bonus, and they are more specific on some very important human issues.

I wrote a book on healing and accidents because health issues are at the forefront of our modern society. The book is a brief guide into the realm of sickness and accidents, and includes some of my own early life experiences and those of others that I have known.

I also included a seven-step book, "Getting Real," which gives those who require more guidance a place to start changes in their lives.

I have always believed that the shortest distance between two points is a straight line, and the fastest way to get what one desires is by knowing that you already have it, or that you are already there.

Within the circumstances that most of us live and accept in the physical world, the simplest of all is 'creating.' Ultimately, this becomes the most difficult because of the limitations we put on ourselves.

As we accept the limitations of others, and make them our new truth, we deny ourselves. We also deny the awesome power that we possess, and we live in fear of using it.

This book is written simply so that little can be left for misinterpretation. Sometimes the message may sound arrogant, impersonal, and unfeeling. I do no make you feel those things, only you do. The information that I present is not exclusive to anyone, it works for everyone. There are no qualifications, no rituals, no promises, and no exercises. The whole book screams out for acceptance of the principals put forward.

Somewhere in the book something will resonate with you, and trigger a physical feeling that leads to a new revelation in your awareness. You will think, "yes, that's it, that makes sense."

I invite you to read the book with an open mind and do not look for anything. The message is in between the lines of text and you will not find it by looking. It will be there for you when you are ready to receive it, and within your own ability to handle and accept the consequences of your new awareness.

I especially ask that you do not make this your new bible. Use it as a stepping stone to move past the awareness presented herein.

Use this book to give birth to a new thought about who and what you are, and then pass it on. When you are ready to move from your place of being, write a new book that encourages others to do the same.

In love and light
Namaste
Roy E. Klienwachter

About The Author

Roy Ernest Klienwachter was born in 1948 in the City of Vancouver, in the beautiful province of British Columbia, Canada.  Most of his foot prints can be traced within the area of the lower mainland of the Fraser Valley. The Fraser River flows from the central interior of the province into this narrow valley off the Pacific Ocean and is world famous as the *Mighty Fraser River*.

Roy was born into a rural family with an older brother and a younger sister. His father died of a logging accident when Roy was just over a year old. His mother raised the children on her own, (on a meager government pension) and never remarried until after his siblings had left home. Roy likes to quip about his mother running away from home to get married, when he was in his 21st year.

During the early years, with all the family at home, they lived in poverty. Roy and his brother took on odd jobs after school and on weekends in a small farming community called Agassiz. The days of cleaning out barns, milking cows, and lifting heavy hay bails brought in much-needed money to buy school supplies and clothes.

Roy sees that part of his childhood as healthy and rewarding. He always had a bit of cash in his pocket, and the physical work added muscle to his skinny frame. When asked, Roy laughs about his impoverished childhood and says that he and his siblings used to fight the dog for table scraps.

Roy was drawn to the typewriter at an early age. A minister at the local Anglican Church would allow him play with the old machine in his office on infrequent visits. Roy loved the typewriter because it represented abundance to him. The machine always had lots of A's, B's and C's. It never ran out no matter how many times he pressed the keys. It was a magnificent letter factory. He spent most of his time filling pages with letters and words, enchanted by the sound that it made.

Roy's first attempt at writing a book happened when he was just nine years old. He was given a printer's set for his birthday. The set consisted of small rubber letters that one assembled in a wooden block or stamp. There was enough room to get three short sentences onto the block. His very first master piece was three or four quarter pages stapled together. It took him most of the day to create it.

He was especially proud of his work and presented it to his mother for much anticipated praise. Her response was not what he expected. She laughed at him and told him how silly he was. She said he couldn't possibly know anything about the subject of his new book. Suffering from wounded pride and disgrace he took her criticism to heart and never wrote anything on paper, except when called upon to do so in school, and then most reluctantly.

At age 15 the family moved closer to the coast into another rural community near the city of Vancouver. During his high school days, Roy went to work for an electronics firm as a technician. He loved electricity and enjoyed repairing anything that was electrical. He worked, periodically for the same company for more than 25 years.

In-between jobs included a wide range of side occupations. For many years he was a professional drummer in a band. He tried his hand at fur trapping and gas fitting. He started several businesses over the years. After 15 years in a most successful business Roy closed the doors, to retire and develop himself spiritually. The following five years were devoted to reading and writing again. His favourite genre is New Age Spirituality, and this is what he now spends most of his time writing about. Roy is fascinated with the process of physical manifesting. He spends his time learning to understand and recreate the process. It is not enough to know that he can do it. He has an insatiable desire to know how the system can be used on a conscious level to create on demand anything that one desires. Roy believes that this comes from his natural desire to know how things work. It is in harmony with his ability to repair things using the gifts that were given to him.

Many of his articles may be found in newspapers and their archives. Some may be seen in popular ezines and on web sites.

Roy has produced a reference CD and several books on New Age Spirituality.

Today, writing is his main aspiration. It is his sincere desire to pass on what he has learned about spirituality and manifesting to those that are ready to move forward with their lives. This book is the merging and revised additions of four of those books. It was created in the hope that it will inspire people to become seekers and move on. Roy's fond wish is that his books will motivate others to create a book that will change the way the all people see themselves with respect to each other and there environments. One of his favourite lines is, "You are not alone, and we are all one!"

Roy believes strongly that we all create the circumstances of our lives, and that we are not victims of it. He encourages people to be pro-active in how and what they experience in this lifetime, and others.

Roy likes to make it very clear that he writes for himself. It is his way of expressing himself. He does not like to present himself as an authority on spirituality, but teaches it so that he may learn. He writes from what he believes and is not afraid to put it down on paper. His intentions are simple, and come through strongly with devotion and purpose. His books bring with them a sense of accomplishment for him, knowing that someone else may benefit from what he writes.

Roy says the writing is easy, the proof reading and corrections are painful. He often does not know what he has written until he reads it.

For more than three years he channeled for Joseth, a spirit entity, which came to his pen each morning before breakfast, and is published on his web site at *www.klienwachter.com.*

Roy was brought up Christian and attended many different traditional churches from Catholic to Pentecostal. He no longer belongs to, or claims any affiliations to organized religion. He respectfully acknowledges their place in history and now believes that there is more than what convention can teach.

Another of his favourite sayings is that "it is time for all of us to move out of the box." To explore more fully our potential and our connectiveness to others, this planet and all that is. We are all connected intimately at some level, and are inseparable. The physical earth is a wonderful playground where we are free to express ourselves in anyway that we desire, without fear of retribution or punishment from that which created us. Unconditional love is what we came from, and what we are and what we experience always, in every second of the eternal moment of now.

Roy's message is clear, it is straight forward and it rings loud. You do not have to try and find it. It will come to you if you are open to it. Do not be discouraged if you do not find it the first time. It simply means you are not ready to receive it yet. All things come appropriately to you when you are in the correct time and place. You cannot let something new in while you are holding on so tightly to that which is already known. You cannot receive until you give it away.

This book was written for you. That is why you are reading it now. It is appropriate that you are here at this time, and even if you do not understand at this instant, it will become clear later.

Now open up your mind, and leave yourself open to new possibilities and experiences. Know always that you can throw the book away at any time you desire, or accept the gift that is being offered to you.

Contents

UNDERSTANDING THE FIRST STEPS

Introduction

All of us at some time in our life get stuck in a belief system. As I like to say, we are stuck in a box, with no new information coming in, or we tend to ignore it. We get comfortable with what we know, and are not willing to go through what we perceive as an effort to change.

In order to get out of your box you must first be willing, at least for the moment, to give up on the idea that "the box" is all there is. If you are not prepared to do this, there is very little likelihood of you learning anything different than that which you already know, and there is little chance of any meaningful growth. In the darkness of the box there is no light for anything to blossom.

One of the biggest fears that many people have about learning anything new is that it might nullify anything that they have believed-in before. One often fears that when they change what they have always believed in, it retroactively means they have been living a lie. This fear is so strong, that one will exaggerate any negative reasoning imagined, in favour of maintaining the status quo.

Playing it safe, not rocking the boat and staying in the comfort zone, is better in the minds of some people than the promise of anything gained by developing themselves spiritually in something as abstract as a new or upgraded belief system.

Being open to new possibilities is scary. There is always the lingering thought that we may be punished for transgressing and unable to return to our comfort zone. Our souls may be lost forever and unredeemable.

In opening up and lifting yourself out of the box it is not necessary to assess your old beliefs as right or wrong. That would be incorrect. What you have believed in, or now believe in, is exactly correct for you at this time of your evolution, given your own model of the world. There is no right or wrong; only that which now works for you and that which doesn't work for you. The fear around "change" is real to your ego.

Because your ego lives in the past, and is always threatened by extinction should you learn something new, it fights any move to evolve. You become a referee in an on going tug-of-war.

Just imagine for a moment the picture of the devil (your ego) on one shoulder, and an angel (your spirit) on the other, carrying on a conversation while you listen to them. It is crucial that you recognize the dialogue when it comes up. Become a silent observer and remind yourself that you would not be opening up to something new if it was not your time to do so, and if it was not a benefit for you.

Your life begins on the edge of your comfort zone it doesn't end there. It is now time for you to know who you really are and go past the illusion of the physical body.

"Everything in the world you know is the materialization of something that exists independently of your plane." 1

Life is every-changing and is the only constant in the universe. Where there is no change life can not exist. Life is limited in the box, which is a "closed system" as you would now understand it.

All closed systems are temporary and are limited in scope or function. Your life in the box is the same. Without new ideas coming into the box there is no change, and therefore limited life and possibilities. New ideas and beliefs bring to your life new possibilities for growth and function.

You create who you are in every minute of your physical existence. You are in total control of what you manifest in your life. You can do, or have anything you desire, simply by knowing it is already yours, and by understanding this principal.

Living in the box is nothing more than slow death, while knowledge is freedom and life. Freedom is who you really are and it is your inheritance. Making choices is exercising your freedom.

Most all of us do not know who we really are, other than our name. For most of our lives we live very much the way we were taught by our parents, our schools, our churches, our friends, and what we read about and see on television. We are a

---

1Jane Roberts, "The Seth Material"

product of how others see us, rather than of who we really are. We are modeled after someone else's idea of how we should be.

I do not pretend to know all the answers, and I would be fearful of anyone who said they had them. It is written, "If you see the Buddha walking down the street, run away from him." The Buddha does not set himself up to be worshiped.

What I am offering here is a way to start the change in your life that will give you the freedom to experience, and see only the good things in your sojourn in this world. I would hope that you never adopt all my beliefs as your own. I would hope that you would never make this book, or any other the new bible in your life. It is always the hope of a good teacher that the student will surpass the teacher. I sincerely want you to create your own truth.

All the answers to all the questions you have are deep within you, they have always been there. You did not come to this world to learn anything, but to experience it. The reality of this life cycle is an expression of what you already know to be true, and what you have already experienced in other lifetimes. What I want to give you in this book is an awareness of that which is already yours.

It is my sincere desire that you will evolve past this book and recreate your own life, that you will never again model your life in the way others would have you. It is also my desire that you not only surpass the teacher but become one. Teaching is simply helping others to remember what they already know intuitively. My way is not the only way, it's just another way.

Chapter 1

Why Would I Want To Be Outside the Box?

Why would I want to get out of the box? I am comfortable here I don't see any need to mess with something that is already working for me. My parents told me to leave well enough alone, "If it ain't broke don't fix it."

Congratulations, if the above line is your philosophy and this is your insight into the way you live, you have answered the above question. If you are truly happy with your life and the way you are living now, and you don't hear that little voice in you saying, "there's got to be more to life than this," then there is no need to fix it.

This is the whole thing about awareness; it is about identifying our life's purpose, and then creating the things in our life that will facilitate the experience of that purpose.

What this book offers is an insight into the probabilities of your life, while creating awareness that there is something more than what you have right now. Life is about growth, and change is the only thing that remains constant. If you are feeling a restlessness about moving on, then this book will give you some basics, a starting point on your path to evolutionary and spiritual enlightenment.

I will tell you the "last thing" you will learn on your journey, first. You will not learn it here in this book or any other book. The great secret is that there is nothing to learn. You are not in school to learn anything, you are here to experience everything.

In order to experience the meaning of your life, you must travel inward. All the answers you seek, are found deep inside yourself, which is the place to look. The one thing that is consistent in all the books you will read, all the tapes you will listen to and all the enlightened people you will talk to is to look inside. Your journey is circular. While you are beginning your trip looking outside of yourself, everywhere you turn you will be guided back to yourself. After your trip is over you will discover that you were already where you say you wanted to be. If you can fully understand this, you will experience your journey as shorter.

You will not find the answers by traveling to Tibet and looking for the Great Buddha, or seeking counseling from a guru, or your Ouija board. A psychic cannot enlighten you. You must be aware always to look inside for your truth.

I started to feel a restlessness or awareness later in my life, at around 50 years old. I noticed that all the experiences in my life were repetitions of what I had been doing for years. I had lived this long and not really moved very far along the path. I have discovered over recent years of study and being open to new things that there is no meaning to life, save for the meaning that I give it.

I discovered that the things that happen in my life are the things that I put in place in order to experience a certain aspect of myself. I also discovered that I have complete control over all of it. I do not believe in coincidence or chance. Everything in my life has been manifested by me, that which works for me and that which does not. I also acknowledge that in order to have any say in these events I must take ownership of the circumstances of my life, especially if it something that appears to be out of my control. Should there be something that I do not like, I cannot give it away unless I own it first; otherwise it is not mine to give away. I am not a victim of my circumstances, I am creating them.

The process of manifesting thoughts into physical reality fascinates me. The process is so simple yet so difficult to do. Nothing in life was ever designed to be complicated. It is our ego that makes things difficult. It is our family, friends and the rest of society that constantly tells us we can not do or have a thing. Because we buy into it, it makes things even more difficult. They tell us we must stick with the status quo, don't try to change things, and we believe them. It becomes part of our ideology.

The idea of manifesting wealth, for instance, is an effortless process. It is your mind that makes the process difficult, until you get over the notion that you "don't deserve" or "cannot" have a thing, you will never get it simply because you believe you can't have or do it.

The great secret to manifesting anything in your life is to re-program the file in your head that says you can't have it.

Those that are in the box and want out are kept there by paper chains. If you constantly put out to the universe—you want to get out of the box—it is what will be echoed back to you. You will receive the awareness that you are still wanting and are still in the box. When you know that you are no longer there is when you will be liberated. During the time that you live in the box, you close your eyes to all other possibilities in order to be comfortable. Fear of the unknown is so strong in some that they will give up any personal growth, and ignore the longing in their souls, only to experience over and over again the things that are familiar and comfortable, no matter how unfulfilling it is. This kind of existence is a dead end road for your soul. It will not survive for long in this body. Life always begins on the edge of your comfort zone, and it always moves to the next level. Without movement evolution could not be a fact.

An old man on his dieing bed, and preparing for death, finally realized that he had been dead for 78 years. Only now, in the last few minutes of his physical life, was he experiencing what had been eluding him all his life, the joy of living. Most of us are afraid to live. We view dying as a relief or an end. Because we have been taught that the struggle will be over when we die, we have not realized the "great secret" that we created the struggle in the first place. The struggle was not necessary, and until we change our thought we will take the experience with us.

The irony is that if we don't get it right the first time, we will come back only to experience it time and time again. This is the law of cause and effect or "Karma." There is no place to go. You can't run away because this life is what you chose to experience. At some level it was all your idea.

Why should you get out of the box? You shouldn't! You shouldn't do anything unless that is what you desire, and you believe that it is time to start living the life you were meant to! If, at some level you did not know this you would not be reading this book now. You are already creating the next step in your spiritual growth. You are now being the great manifestor that you imagined yourself to be. You are moving further along the path less traveled and are waking up.

Beware! You can never go back. Having acquired new knowledge and new skills, you will always have an overwhelming desire to experience what you know and put into practice that which you have learned. Having given up your innocence, there is always a natural progression towards that which is even better.

Once you learn how to dance, you will begin to go out and dance. You will want to learn new steps. You will want to experience these new steps with others on the dance floor. You will shine in their presence. They will see how marvelous you are, the new knowledge will manifest beautifully in every step you take. Ever seeking to experience new dances you will begin to teach others the joy of dancing. You will never go back to being a wall flower.

Why Are Some People Afraid of Spirituality?

I don't believe that people are so much afraid of spirituality as they are of the unknown, or of losing what they already have.

Throughout your life from the time you were babies to adulthood, you have been told how to live, how to behave, and what to do in any given situation. You have been molded by others and within the confines of their own understanding or model of the world.

After you were born your parents told you what your name was and that you were a girl or a boy. They gave you their culture and belief systems and, through ignorance, you accepted . They told you what their faith was and you grew up believing as they did. They told you what their politics were and you grew up supporting the same party. Mother told you what detergent to use in the laundry and that has been handed down through generations, in her family and yours.

When you got old enough to start to think on your own, you started to question, and rebel against some of the things they taught you. This brought you into direct conflict with them and you suffered for it. The church told you what to believe, and laid down stiff penalties for not conforming. Your school set out rules to follow, and you learned what happens when you don't comply with them. You know what happens when you don't follow the proper pecking order with your school mates and friends. You are humiliated or driven out of the circle.

Is it any wonder that you may just be a little bit afraid about reaching out to experience something that is not popular in the eyes of those in your life? Your friends also fear for you because they intuitively know that you may leave them behind if you find something better. This is something that I found out from personal experience. You will leave most of them behind.

Take a moment to reflect back to an earlier age during your adolescence. There are things you did that you now think of as immature and you can no longer relate to that level of maturity anymore. It is the same with spiritual growth as you move to another level. You will have difficulty relating to people from a past level of experience, or with those that are evolving slower.

Greater levels of understanding will give you new tools to assess your world and your life. It also brings greater joys, experiences and pleasures. It's similar to learning a new language, those that have not learned will not understand and will move away from you if you continue to use it. While others who know the language will have no problem relating to you and will be drawn to you.

Personal growth often means leaving behind the people you know and love. We all experience this when we leave home for the first time. We just know it is time to move on.

Some churches and organized religions have their own agenda, and would cease to exist if the congregation evolved past their teachings and left. Some religions have laid down stiff penalties for deviating from practiced doctrine, which is designed to thwart any kind of growth beyond the teachings of the church.

Spirituality is an awareness of whom you are internally and the relationship between you, others and your environment. There is nothing to fear about knowing who you are. What you gain is wisdom as you move away from fear. You also start becoming the person you have always intuitively known yourself to be. As you move closer to this inner image of yourself life becomes easier, you will be able to empathize with your ego, and not be affected by its paranoia.

Understanding that you are already in heaven allows you to see the angels. Taking control and responsibility for your life will present you with un-boundless freedom. Freedom is unconditional love and unconditional love is who you really are.

Your past cannot be reasonably used as a sole excuse for the way you turned out or for the way you now live your life. You have total freedom to live it any way you want, not the way others have taught you. You cannot use reasoning that puts the blame on others, or your parents, for the way your life is today. At some level you chose to accept what others have handed to you or expected from you. It is also something that you planned before your birth

You have little control over someone abusing you as a child, but you have total freedom of how you will respond to it or how you will allow it to effect your life. If you do not choose to live the drama, then you have to claim ownership of the event and let it go. In the moment you take ownership of an event you have the power to give the effects of it away. If you do not acknowledge the event, you give that power away to someone or something else.

> "You create yourself entirely through the free choices that you make every day of your life. Though you may try to pretend otherwise, the reality is that you are the originator of your actions, the master of your fate and the captain of your soul, for better or for worse. You may choose to surrender control of your life to other individuals or organizations, but this is ultimately a free choice that you make and for which you are completely responsible."—
> *Jean-Paul Sartre*

Freedom only comes with taking responsibility for your choices. If others are making choices for you then you are not free, you are a living symbol of their expectations or image of you. If you are bound to others by obligation you are not free. In order to have control of what you do you must take ownership of the decision and the consequences. If you are to weed out the things that do not work in your life you cannot get rid of them if you do not own them. Nor should you keep them because you feel obligated to do so.

Obligation to another is the biggest sin you can commit against yourself. It is a denial of who you really are. If you are doing a thing for someone else, whether it be your friend, spouse, or children, and you are doing it because you feel obligated and it goes against who you really are; you are denying yourself and have created the biggest blasphemy. Do not a thing because you feel obligated. Do it because it declares who you are at that moment, and the thing that you are doing is a symbol of that thought process and an expression of who you know yourself to be. In other words if a person holds out his hand to you, help him only if you see yourself as a helping person. Do not help because you feel guilty or obligated. If helping is not something you would normally do, then doing something for another because of guilt denies who you really are, which is a person who normally does nothing to help. Do not act out of fear.

Fear is present in our lives because we keep it there. Moving along the spiritual path of enlightenment brings us farther away from fear. Fear is the exact opposite of love. A person who does not love oneself is living in fear. Spirituality is not about fear it is about whom you really are, that which is the opposite of fear, that which is love.

> *Fear is at the opposite end of the stick. The farther we move away from love, the more fearful we become. The farther we move away from fear, the more loving we become. Love and fear akin to each other.*

In the absolute there is no fear. Fear is relative and only exists in the physical world. The concept of fear was created so that you could experience love. This movement is a natural rhythm or expression in time and space.

When you act from obligation you are not acting from love but from fear. You are not expressing who you really are. In order to give love unconditionally you must truly love yourself first. When you know yourself as a truly loving person you can give to anyone freely from love, not from a sense of obligation. Obligation always comes from the point of fear.

Why Are There So Many Belief Systems?

Choice is freedom, absolute freedom is unconditional love and unconditional love is who you really are. This is the great secret which the human species seems to overlook.

Unconditional love has no conditions attached to it. Absolute freedom of love allows for multiplicity and diversity or choice.

It is ironic that the greatest thing we have on this planet is diversity of plant life, animal life, human life, cultures, languages, seasons and landscapes. This is our greatest strength, and yet it is also the one thing that you have the least tolerance for.

If someone does not dress the same way you do, she is outcast. If another eats a different kind of food than you or is a vegetarian or eats meat or a certain kind of meat, they are driven out or ridiculed for their preference. Now if they are a different colour they are exploited or killed. Should this person be female, they are likely to be treated as second class citizens. If they have a different religion or belief system they will not go to heaven, some will even kill because of their different beliefs.

The root cause of these reactions is the fear of loosing your identity, causing you to defend who you think you are. Your ego is who you belief yourself to be, the five sensory personality that you can see and touch. Your ego is very fragile and believes at any moment it could become extinct. When it senses something different from what it knows to be true or different than itself, alarm signals go off. The ego can not live in the present moment but lives in the past or future. A new thought that is different from yours is an instant threat to its existence.

It is a paradox that your ego doesn't like change or things that it cannot relate to outside of its own paradigm, yet it goes out of its way to be different. It is your nature to express your individuality; you would think that ego would be anxious to be assimilated. It is the separation from each other that creates anxiety about perceived differences.

A boiling pot of water and ketchup added does not make for a great bowl of soup. However, when you add vegetables, meat and spices, you create something even better. Any time you add something new to the pot it becomes something different than it was before. Different combinations give different results, some better some not. The whole becomes greater than its parts.

You often use the phrase, "two heads are better than one." Why? No one person has all the answers, no one person has ever been able to create the perfect mix. Someone else will come along and add something new and it becomes the next best mix.

Diversity is the one greatest gift that has been given to mankind, and yet it is not seen that way by many, or even most. Diversity in your belief systems should be your greatest strength; they are all different paths to the same place.

There is no one way that is the only way or the best way, all roads converge and each way offers an infinite variety of choices to experience yourself differently from any other way. Each one is the mother lode, unique and rich in its possibilities.

There is more than one name for the creator; Adonai, Allah, Elohim, God, Hari, Jehovah, Krishna, Lord, Rama, Vishnu, Yahwey, plus a few more. There is no lack of names for that which created us.

Our understanding of who the creator is, is taught to us through many books: The Bible, Qur'an, Book of Mormon, Bhagavad-Gita, Torah,

Veda, Lun-yu, Pali Canon, Hadith, Upanishad, I Ching, Adi Granth, Mahabharata, Yoga-sutras, Mathnawi, Kojiki. They are all mans' interpretations of how humanity thinks God wants you to live.

All these religious books share many common beliefs. The one that stands out the most is fear. Most are based on the fear of humanities own extinction. Along with man's extinction these books have created religions with agendas that include, first and foremost, a guaranty for their own survival. They have built into them safeguards, punishments, even death for deviating from the sacred scriptures. Religions have created separation from the believers, unbelievers and deviates. They have separated man from God, man from man, and man from woman. They have all missed the point.

"We are all one," we were put here to experience ourselves in as many ways as possible, every possible aspect of ourselves that we can recreate. We were given freedom of choice in order to be able to do that. The diversity of thought that is shown in the different religions and religious books is testament of our unlimited ability to express ourselves differently and yet be in harmony with the one most common truth, there is only one consciousness, one creator of which we are all part and of which we will all return.

Religion and, in particular man's ego have tried to make the separation in order to assure their own survival. The ego is not all that you are, this is a great truth. The fear that accompanies the illusion of separation is expressed throughout the world in our intolerance of those who do not believe as we do. Through ongoing spiritual evolution, the fear disappears with the knowingness that there really is only one spirit, the spirit of the creator, and you are all connected to that spirit. It is the pain of separation that drives you to seek the answers in as many ways as possible.

You are as waves upon the ocean. You are individualized pieces of the same thing with your own personality, yet still connected to each other with all the attributes and characteristics of the whole.

Why Am I Here?

I have created a very simplistic explanation of why you are here. This is yet another theory in a world full of theories and it is no better or worse than any other theory. *"My way is not the only way, it's just another way."* You, as disembodied souls of God, cannot return to the oneness of the creator until you recreate all the probabilities. Life is purposeful, and was created especially for you to recreate yourself as a part of the wholeness of God. You have a divine destiny to recreate the body of your creator that he may know himself experientially.

One of the best ways to be enlightened is to teach what you want to know. That is what I am doing here, now. I don't pretend to know all the answers. I'm teaching what I now know. I am also learning from those I teach. All the secrets of the creator are already known to me, at some level of my consciousness.

A good teacher does not try to teach anything, but helps the student remember what she already knows. Teaching helps you remember what you already know, and develop it further. Once you finish this book start to teach what you've learned, and new probabilities will present themselves to you.

The "big bang theory" is one that has been around for some time and is believed by many. It can neither proven nor can it be disproved. It is another probability. I'm not asking you to believe it; it is used here to possibly explain your relationship to the creator. It is designed to help you get started on the path to your own theory or understanding. It is a kick start for you, motivation to explore other probabilities. This is one possible explanation and perhaps your reason for being here.

For a moment, imagine that you have spent the last seven years studying to be a lawyer. You worked very hard to become the best in your class and the best lawyer that ever was. You got perfect marks and you were the head of your class. No one ever reached as high as you and made it. You graduated with honours and have all kinds of offers from major law firms. You have known all along that you are a great lawyer, now you yearn to experience yourself as that lawyer. You have an overwhelming urge to experience what "best" means in relationship.

The hardest part of this job is going to be choosing between the best firms or starting your own practice. Because you are such a high achiever you will need stimuli that will befit someone of your stature. You need a position that will reflect the high marks that you have earned. You must now decide how you will experience your life as the best lawyer.

Now, imagine yourself as God. As God you are all perfect you exist everywhere, you are all powerful and you have no fear, you are all that is so there is no other to fear. There is nothing that you need because you are everything, and because you are everything there is nothing that you want. You are absolute magnificence and perfection. In the world of the absolute there can be nothing other than perfection and no way to relate to it. Perfection is also the end of creativity. That which is perfect can not be changed, it is perfected.

Now you have the same dilemma as the lawyer. You have awareness but you long to experience yourself in all your excellence. Knowing is not enough you must now experience perfection. How are you going to do it?

After pondering this impasse for some time as God, you came up with a brilliant idea. In order to experience that which is perfect you must be able to experience its opposite, that which is not perfect. You must create relativity. There must be a situation where you can experience all the things that you are not, in order to experience all the things that you are. How could such a thing come to pass? What would be the venue for such an occurrence?

It was God's creative genius to divide itself up into smaller pieces. By doing this each of its individualized parts could look back on the whole through time and space, thus creating relativity. Now each piece of the whole would know itself relevant to the one (all there is) and could relate back to the whole through the life force that runs through it, all parts being atomically connected to all other individualized parts.

Because God is omnipresent this created another problem; where would this happen? Having no other place for this to happen because God is all there is. God had to make this happen within his own body. God literally exploded (the big bang theory) into an infinite number of pieces forcing themselves outward within his own body to create the universe. Each piece being an individualized piece of God, the re-creative process could now begin to take place in the new physical universe relative to the whole.

Man is made in the image of God, with all the attributes and properties of God. In order to recreate himself in all aspects of himself through man, God gave man free will to do, or recreate anything that came to his mind. Relative to God, man has come up with all the things that we do not associate with what God is, and is not.

Man imagined Hell (where God is not) and created it in his head. This gives relativity to Heaven (where God dwells) which he also created in his mind. Neither one of these places exists except in your imagination, they are concepts. Both places exist for us now, here in the place and time that we are conscious of. Man also created evil so that he may know good. Therefore the myth of original sin now becomes the original blessing.

God could not do all this without you; you are here to recreate yourself in every moment of now! By recreating yourself you are recreating who God is; it is God recreating God through himself. Through this process God will know himself as perfect because, through you, he will know himself as not perfect. Once this cycle is completed the universe will cave back into itself. There are already suggestions that it may be occurring now. Once the energy of an explosion is exhausted it falls back into itself. At that time you will be back with the whole and the process will start over again.

Chapter 2

When Do I Start?

You already started the process when you were born, you may not have been aware of it but you did start. You will get as many chances as you need to experience all that you want, until you experience all that there is to experience in this dimension, the three dimensional physical world.

In this life, or any other, there is nothing you have to say, do or be, except exactly what you are being right now. You are perfect the way you are. We are all unique and have a special purpose for being here; there is something that only you can do in this consciousness that will add to the greater awareness. You may experience life consciously, or unconsciously, as you prefer and it is always a choice.

There are only two ways you can travel through this lifetime. You can be aware and interactive in co-creating this life cycle, or you can be unaware and go along for the ride. Either way is acceptable and you need not apologize for your choice. You can exercise your freedom to choose what you will experience or take what's handed to you, either way you will not be judged by God.

Having read this far into the book was not by happenstance and at some level you were drawn to it. You picked it up or chose to bring it into your life, not by accident but intentionally. This was the one possibility that you chose from an infinite sea of probabilities. You are already aware that there is something else and that is why you are reading this now. This is the way it happens. You cannot deny that which you know to be true. You will make the same choice again as you read on.

When you are ready your life starts opening up to the new probabilities. Everything that you need for your next experience is presented to you. Choose carefully.

I have many books in my library. Some of them I purchased four years ago and have not read them yet. Some of the newest books I have read first. When I finish reading a book I go back to my library and, most of the time, I do not know what I am looking for, nor do I have any particular preference. The book that is timely for me to read is already there, and usually answers some questions that have recently come up, or it is on a topic that will come up in my wisdom circle. Seldom do we plan ahead what we want to discuss, so it is truly amazing when I pick up a book that covers the topic of our discussion.

Once you start opening up to the new possibilities, people will start showing up in your life that understand your new enlightenment and are there to help you. There are no chance meetings. It may simply be a smile from a stranger, but they will be there. When the student is ready, the master will come.

When Will I Be Enlightened?

The answer is, "probably not in this lifetime!" I would also add be "wary" of the one who says he is enlightened for he is a false profit. Enlightenment is a process, not an end unto itself. It is not a place that you get to. In all ways you are becoming enlightened, you can never be enlightened. Life is a process and it is always changing. Every new thought you have, changes your life at some level and recreates that which you are. You are not even the same person that started reading this book, you have already changed. The level of your existence that you are now aware of is not the only one. You exist in an infinite number of probabilities, and they are all valid forms and exist simultaneously.

To be enlightened you would have to know yourself as the creator. You would have to know all that the creator knows and at that point your true identity would be revealed to you, your rightful heritage would be known to you, you would be enlightened.

It is written that in the Christian history of this planet, only a few men have achieved enlightenment in this version of your life, which you are now experiencing. Jesus, Enoch, Moses, Elijah, Isaiah are the only ones mentioned in the Bible that were transformed.

Enlightenment is a process of moving into knowingness of who you are. It is not something that you have to achieve. You either know yourself to be enlightened or you know yourself trying to achieve enlightenment. The transformation of Jesus, Enoch, Moses, Elijah and Isaiah came with enlightenment.

As you move into higher levels of enlightenment the atoms of your physical body speed up gradually transforming you from the physical to the non-physical. Death is also a human convention. Man was never meant to die, but to transform.

Transformation from the physical back to the oneness of the creator is the result of enlightenment. Death does not take us there. Death brings us back here or to some other realm, where we can experience our enlightenment and move further along the path. Enlightenment is an illusion; we in fact are all enlightened creatures. At some level we hold all the secrets to creation, we have only to remember and we will experience instant enlightenment.

When Will I Know I'm on the Path?

This is one of the ironies or paradoxes of your sojourn in this lifetime. You will not know that you are on the path until you realize that you are not.

We are here in the physical world because this is the only place that we can experience ourselves through our five senses in three dimensions in a relative world. This is the only place that we can experience hot because we can experience cold. We can know one because we can experience the other. If we were in a place that was always hot, eventually we would not be able to experience it because we would not have its opposite to remind us.

Experience is not an element of the absolute and knowing all that there is, is not the same as experiencing it. That is why you came to this planet, to be able to experience all that you know. So that the creator could experience all that it knows through you. Without you it would not be possible for the creator to experience anything that there is. That is why you are here, that is why you came, not to know but to experience.

Being in the physical, relative world gives us the opportunity to experience being on the path to enlightenment, because in this world, for most of the time, we are not on the path.

The path to enlightenment is a continuous process of remembering, re-member-ing, (putting the pieces back together) of who you really are. If you know yourself as, or have an image of yourself as being, a generous person for example, and an opportunity comes along for you to demonstrate your generosity and you don't, you will know that you have moved off the path. If you are conscious of this the next time the opportunity comes along, you will demonstrate your generosity. This is another example of cause and effect (Karma).

The concept of karmic debt is a knowingness that you are off the path, and acknowledgement of a mistake and a correction by then getting back onto the path; it's not actually a collection of misdemeanors for which you recompense. So called Karmic debt can be nullified with an awareness of moving back onto the spiritual path.

If you believe yourself to be an honest person and then at income tax time, for example, you knowingly cheat or omit something on your return, you are not demonstrating your honesty; you have moved off the path or created a karmic debt.

To repay the debt is as simple as moving back onto the path and becoming honest again.

Every time you make a decision to do something that is not in accord with who you know yourself to be, you move off the path. This cannot be taken lightly you cannot fool yourself. A pattern of moving off and on the path is also a mistake. This also demonstrates who you really are. There is no penalty or punishment handed out by the universe for moving off the path. You will simply know yourself again as one who is not on it, and you make a correction. Knowingness or enlightenment does not come by trying to fool yourself. You can lie to yourself, but at some level you will know the truth and you will remember it.

You are always what you demonstrate; your thought word and deed are symbols of where you are along the spiritual path of enlightenment. Every time you demonstrate something other than what you know yourself to be, you can say you have wandered off the path. These symbols are sign posts that say "hey, you're going in a direction that is not working for you, considering where you say you want to go, turn here and get back on the path.

The path to enlightenment is one you follow alone. It is a solitary journey. In this world there are more than six billion individuals following their own paths. Only you know what it is you want to experience, and who you believe yourself to be or what your purpose is. You are not only an individual, but so is your purpose. It is unique, and only you can experience it.

Every step you take is observable by the symbols you leave behind, and it clearly demonstrates whether you are on the path that you have chosen. It does no good to talk the talk, sooner or later you must walk the walk. If not in this lifetime then you will have another chance, and another, until you have completed your journey and reached enlightenment. Then you have gone full circle and are back with the creator. You cannot fool yourself ever. or anyone else for that matter, for whom else would there be to fool if we are all one?

It is the natural tendency of all souls to move to the next higher level of understanding. This being a given, what would you gain by trying to fool or lie to yourself? It simply means a delay along the road that leads to your fulfillment. Is it not more gratifying to notice that you have strayed, make a correction and thus demonstrate your awareness? This can only come from being self aware and more enlightened.

Chapter 3

Where Do I Start?

There is no one place to start that is better than another. It started for me when I was given a book to read. It was the trigger that got me reading more books, and once I started I didn't want to stop. It could easily have been a casual conversation with someone, or an event that I may have witnessed. It was a book that was given to me on loan to read. I did not mention to anyone that I wanted to read a book. I haven't read more than a handful of books since I finished high school. This was a synchronistic opportunity, and was the medium or catalyst that inspired me to look further and start reading again.

It doesn't really matter what the circumstances when the time comes, you will know. My first thoughts were, "that sounds interesting," and then, "that makes sense to me," and then, "maybe there is something to all this." When I left myself open to learn something new it all started happening.

I must state it again here, the last thing you will learn is that you had the knowledge all along, you just weren't aware of it. The place to start is within. Every answer to every question you ever had is buried deep inside you. A great teacher knows this and helps the student to remember what they already know to access the infinite knowledge within.

Let intuition guide you in your everyday affairs. There is a learning curve in the process of trusting your intuition. You will make some mistakes until you get comfortable with what you are feeling, and then it will become the natural thing to do. Your intuition is most often the very first thought you have about something before the brain starts to reason. Once the brain gets involved   the opportunity is lost.

The C.E.O. and founder of the Sony Corporation never went to business school and yet he was worth billions. His secret was, when he received a business proposal, he ate it. If it came back up he turned it down. He relied entirely on intuition to make his business decisions and fortune. He relied on the feeling in his stomach, the knowingness that lies within waiting for us to call upon its resources.

Meditation is the preferred method of getting in touch with your spirit or inner self. There is a wealth of information in books and spiritual organizations as to the benefits of continuing meditation—not only for the physical body, but for getting in touch with the others two-thirds of who you are.

Being the captain of your ship will not get you very far if you're not able to communicate with the rest of your crew. Likewise, you must know what it is that your spirit wants to experience in order to be in harmony with your purpose here. You are a three part being; body, mind and spirit. Somewhere along the way you are going to trip over each other if you don't communicate.

At the back of this book I have included some information on organizations as well as some titles of a few books that I have read and believe to be very helpful. I have visited the web sites; they are an excellent place for you to start. You can review a more comprehensive list, posted on my web site at *www.klienwachter.com.*

Www.klienwachter.com is another great place to start your journey. There are some very good articles posted in Roy Bits, and you can check out the archives for past articles.

Where Do I Go To Meet Others Who Are Like Minded?

Finding others that are of like mind was difficult for me when I started to expand my awareness into spirituality. I didn't know where to look or whom to talk to. I thought about wearing something that said, hey look I'm into spirituality—do you want to talk about it? I now believe this is a common mistake that one makes. We don't look for spiritual people they find us. Later when I gave up on the idea of finding any, an amazing thing happened; people just started popping up all over. Opportunities for them to find me began showing up in some of the most unexpected places.

I finished reading a book about wisdom circles and I thought that it would be a great idea to start my own circle. Once again I was reminded; I didn't know anyone to ask. About three days later I had a chance encounter with an acquaintance who had dropped into the library. She lived in a neighbouring city and seldom ever came to my library. Before that chance meeting we never said more than a few words to each other and certainly nothing personal.

During our conversation she brought up the idea of starting a group to discuss spirituality. This was an amazing synchronistic experience; we decided to start a wisdom circle at my local library. We agreed to meet at the library on the following weekend to go over details.

For more information on this topic see "wisdom circles" on my site at *www.klienwachter.com.*

The wisdom circle started with no fanfare and with its only two members—Vicky and I. We sat in the library lounge talking about how we were going to organize the circle. We must have been talking too loudly because a young man (David) overheard us and asked us if he could join the group. A few minutes later yet another man (Robin) asked to be included. Like magic the circle was formed in less than an hour. The following week a young lady named Gabriella, who takes care of the plants in the library, overheard us and asked if she could be included.

Others have come into the circle the same way. They have very much the same story. They have been looking but could not find anyone to talk to about spirituality. They were afraid to talk to their friends or anyone close to them for fear of being rejected or just misunderstood. None of them were looking when they came into contact with the circle. They were all chance meetings, at the right place and the right time. When the student is ready the teacher will appear, and nothing is by chance.

The web is a great place to chat with people of like mind. There are many chat rooms to choose from. I didn't like my experiences with chat rooms. They seemed to get pretty gossipy and some just went on and on about little or nothing. I have stayed away from the chat rooms for the most part, and look for useful information that has some relevancy from the site.

Some of the spiritual book authors have great websites. They have invested much of their publishing earnings into courses and retreats, which they offer to you from their sites. Neale Donald Walsch is one such author who goes beyond writing books and walks the walk in his daily life. There is a link to his site from mine at klienwachter.com. I also welcome feedback and email at my site.

Where Can I Get Publications and Material on Spiritualism?

People and spiritual material go hand and hand, so anyplace you find spiritual people they will have material. One of the things that many of these people have in common is that they read a lot, and are always willing to pass on information about great books they have read.

Books on the subject are readily available; please refer to my book list on my site. I suggest looking on the web for used books first. I have listed some places that specialize in used books on my site. Indigo, Amazon, Barnes and Noble are good sites for new books and magazines.

It is apparent that all web sites want you on their lists and will email you weekly or monthly ezines at no charge. One of my favourite local Vancouver paper magazines is Common Ground; it's a great all-round New Age or New Thought spiritual magazine.

Since the sixties there has been an ever increasing glut of New Age, New Thought and self help books presented to an eagerly-awaiting public market. There are so many books, in fact, that it is sometimes overwhelming and difficult to just pick up a book and buy it based on the cover alone.

If you are not sure about the author or the books check out the dust covers, inside front and back, for endorsements. If one of my favourite authors has put their name on a book as an endorsement, I will usually take a chance on it. I do not suggest that you use this method alone as you will limit yourself, and miss out on some other great books or magazines. Scan through the introduction to gain some insight into what the author has to offer.

I believe it is best to have a diversity of thoughts and opinions from as many authors as possible. Some writers can be very biased, therefore it is best to read books by a variety of authors. My writing is a culmination of many authors. Their thoughts and ideas have melded with mine into a uniquely moulded belief system that is mine. Make no book your new bible! Use all that you learn as a stepping stone to something that is even better. After all, you are making all this up.

Understanding spiritual concepts come in sudden bursts or as a new revelation to me. I may read about a thing, I may even understand it, but it has not yet formed my truth. Several weeks may go by and I may even write about what I've learned. Then out of the blue, when it is least expected, the idea will pop into my head as a new idea or thought and I'll think, "that's it, now I understand fully," and its becomes my new reality. Not surprisingly I have talked to others and they have also mentioned similar occurrences. You can also expect these kinds of occurrences along your journey.

Chapter 4

Who Is Right?

Right or wrong is not part of the big picture—it never was. It is a human concept developed to guide people along a path created in the minds of men for mankind. A system of good and bad, right and wrong, was imposed upon populations as a guide and a means of controlling human behavior. This was not a God-created convention. Man was incorrect in believing that God ever intended for us to follow any rules about God. *I often use "man" because it was man that created Christianity as he struggled to take away the power from a matriarchal society.*

The creator gave unconditional love and freedom and it means just that, no conditions and no rules. Conditional love was never what God intended. Conditional love is not consistent with absolute freedom of choice. Rules came along later, of course, and were created by man in accordance with what he thought God wanted of us. He misunderstood again. If God is all powerful what is it that we have that God alone could not get just by making it so? It is a mistake to believe that God must have wanted something in the first place.

The separation in time and space from the love of the creator was created by man through necessity. The creator could never have mapped out a clear path for humanity to follow; it would have defeated the whole purpose of us being here, and the reason for our individuality.

Creativity is our very essence—it is what we are here to do—to create! Life is all about creating and experiencing, nothing more. Only through "free will" does it become possible for the creator to experience itself as all aspects of itself.

There are those who would argue that mankind could never exist without rules. Otherwise, we would have anarchy. They may be correct. Given the way that we have chosen to live our lives so far, it would certainly seem that way. It is not that it is impossible to live without rules; it is just that civilization is not there yet. At one time we did, and some small tribes still live that way.

In a highly enlightened society very few rules would be necessary. In such a society we would become observers and do only those things that work for the betterment of society because that makes sense. We would not repeat the mistakes of past generations for that would be considered insanity, and that which works and that which doesn't work is always observable. Only humanity keeps hitting itself over the head with the same hammer, on the same spot, and this is also observable.

> If you can follow this, you will understand the paradox.
>
> There cannot be only one right way. The only possible way to experience the only right way is to experience another right way that is not the only right way, otherwise there would be nothing else, except the only right way, and that could not be experienced as the only right way.

"All ways" have relevancy within the context of that which works and that which doesn't. Considering your model of the world, and who you know yourself to be, there can never be a wrong way, there can only be your way and your way is not the only way—your way is just another way.

There are laws of nature that have serious consequences should you try and go against them. For instance, if you jump naked off the side of a 2000 foot cliff onto the rocks, you will die. In the physical world of mankind I believe there are no consequences, there are only punishments.

Consequences are natural occurrences that happen when you go against a law of nature. Punishment is man-made and they are put upon us by humanity because we have not followed the rules, or broken a law.

There are no rules to follow when developing spiritual enlightenment. How could there be when you are making all this up as you go along? What I am giving you in this book is a guideline, a place to start. There is no church, no organization, no bible, no author, no man nor women that is right.

Should anyone tell you that they are or that their book is "the only way," turn away from them, they are false prophets.

The truth about your life is who you are at any given moment. It is not even who you were a moment ago or who you will be a moment from now. You are living proof of your existence and you are living your truth in this moment that is now. Your life is a symbol of where you are spiritually. Being on the tenth rung of the ladder does not make you any better than someone who is on the first rung. We all started there and it is continuous.

The moral idea of "right" is the worst belief that has ever been visited upon man. It is the first credence that has separated mankind from its creator and each other. You can feel free to explore your spirituality any way you wish without fear of being wrong or punished by the creator. It is in breaking the laws of man that brings punishment upon you.

If you choose a way that goes against what your spirit wants to experience, than you will simply know that what you have chosen doesn't work for you. You will know this because you will not get what you desire.

The "Categorical Imperative," was created by a well known German philosopher, Immanual Kant.

Kant says that it is neither ethical nor moral to use people as a "means to an end." You must treat them as "ends." You must allow that people are able to make a decision based on the information at hand. It is unethical to manipulate, bribe or coerce people as a means to an end even if you believe that it is in their best interests.

Unlike personal preferences or taste, morals are expressed as you would have it, as a "universal truth," and it must be open to reason in the public arena. In others words, if I told you that it is immoral to kill, I am not saying that it is just immoral for me to kill, but for everyone. I can give logical reasons for wanting it to be a universal morality such as, if we all killed each other off there would be no one left, the species would not survive.

If I told you, on the other hand, that I liked ice cream and you asked me why I may not be able to explain why I like it, except to say I like the taste. That is a perfectly acceptable explanation, and this is a expression of personal preference, and it does not have to be a universal truth, or reasoned and put up for public debate.

Ethical views are primarily statements of reason not expressions of emotion. It is not ethical to force another to accept any moral view without question. It does not work to say something is right or something is wrong, ethical or moral statements must be supported by reasons and aired in a public forum.

If you agree with Kant's Imperative then what the churches have been doing for thousands of years have be unethical if not immoral.

Who Is In Control?

There has always been only one person in control of your life, and that is you. You orchestrated all the events of your life from the time of your birth until your death, you will have manifested every occurrence and circumstance, both good and bad, or what works and what doesn't work. This is what I've been trying to tell you, there is no one else. You have masterminded the whole thing. If you did not experience what it was that you desired in this lifetime you will return and have another opportunity to do it again and again, as many times as needed. You are the captain and this is your ship. This is the unconditional love that the creator gave you; love that is forgiving for as many times as it takes. How many times would a parent allow a child to make the same mistakes before it was abandoned?

Most of you give up your freedom for comfort and security, or to fit into the status quo. What little freedom you may have experienced during a short period between adolescence and adulthood you have given up in order to fit into the image that your parents, friends and society had for you.

You are still navigating the endless probabilities that face you each and every day. But you are not doing it in a way that is in harmony with what your spirit wants to experience. "Free will," often gets in the way of your spirits desires. Objectively, free will is both your blessing and your curse. Your free will most often choose the safe way, the way that others have gone before, the road most traveled.

Whom or What Do You Believe, Is In Control of Any Part of Your Life Now?

Tick off your answers in the boxes below.

€ Me
€ Spouse or significant other
€ Children
€ One of your parents
€ Friends
€ Church
€ Boss
€ Beliefs
€ Sibling
€ Trends
€ Addictions
€ TV
€ Money
€ Bills
€ Debt
€ Fantasy
€ Obligation
€ Government
€ Incarceration
€ Illness
€ Sex
€ Poverty

If you have ticked off any one of the squares other than "me," you are not in complete control of your life. You have given up part of your freedom for that element you feel you have no control over. If you can walk away from any one of these things without regret, then you were in control before you committed, and it is not an obligation but an expression or symbol of who you are.

Chapter 5

What Is Religion?

From the Collins Dictionary it reads; belief in worship of, or obedience to a supernatural power or powers considered to be divine or to have control of human destiny.

Christian religion itself rests its greatest hope on the assurance that man rises from the dead. He passes from this plane to the next, retaining and carrying with him into the beyond those qualities and attributes which constitute that personal flow of consciousness known as an individual.2

Acceptance of proof is the fundamental characteristic of western religion. The function of eastern religion is to allow the mind to escape the confines of the symbolic.3

Christianity accounts for about one-third of the world's population. Islam has about one-fifth of the world's population as followers; and Atheists account for another one-fifth of the world's population. Bahai', Buddhism, Confucianism, Judaism, Taoism and others claim the rest.

All the major religions have been born or prefigured in dreams. There is no true religion. All religions are based on man's idea of God and are subject to his whims and the circumstances of the

2 *Science of Mind by, Ernest Holms Page 386*
3 *The Dancing Wu Li Masters by, Gary Zukav Page 310*

time the religion was conceived. Religions are man's ideas of how God would have us live.

Belief systems come and go, as does the tide, and most things dreamed up by man. These are man's creations and not something constructed by God. They are nurtured by His curiosity, creative nature and willingness to push the boundaries of His own existence.

Religions purport to be a statement of God's preferences, but God doesn't have preferences. To say that God does not have the will or power to impose His preferences, if he had any, would be to say that He is a lesser God, or impotent. True religion is not a withdrawal from the world, but knowledge of the imminence of God in all creation. All true religions would build a bridge to God, not a wall.

Opportunity, not obligation, is the corner stone of any meaningful religion, the basis of all spirituality. Mankind missed the point in many cases. Nothing divides humanity more than language, culture or religion. Religions have made God the "Great Mystery," and caused you not to love God, but to fear God. Religion has separated man from man, women from women, man from women and man from God. Some religions actually tell man that he is above women. It is religion that has set the church in the roll of an intermediary in order to reach God.

What Is Spiritualality?

In his book, "Edgar Cayce, On Channeling your Higher Self," Author Henry Reed writes, that spiritualism had its start on March 31st 1848 in New York City, with simple raps on the walls from a disembodied spirit in the Fox household.

From the Collins dictionary, "the state or quality of being dedicated to God, religion, or spiritual things or values, esp. as contrasted with material or temporal ones."

The fields of New Thought or New Age spiritualism may include religion and the church. It does not take away from it, but adds to the quality of religion and faith. It is, however, an approach or philosophy that does not always include the doctrines of organized religion.

I believe that spirituality is the study of who we really are. I strongly believe that we are part of a superior thought process or intelligence, exclusive of our physical bodies. We are a three-part being made up of mind, spirit and body. Mind is the creator, spirit is the part of the creator that gives us life, and body is the physical or the ego.

It is our ego that is conscious, and what we know ourselves to be, and it is the part that has free will. It is the ego that our parents raised and society moulded into what is perceived by those around us. But it is not who we really are, it is an illusion, and only one third of the triune of mind, body and spirit.

We are spirit, naturally, and there is no place that we have to look for spirituality, it is what we are. Spirituality is non-denominational and non-partisan, it is inclusive of and transcends all religious boundaries. It is the science of exploring our relationship with that which created us and that which the creator is, and how it is evolving. It is not a rigid contracted view of a static, anthropomorphic being, which lays down unrealistic laws for us to follow and passes out one-way trips to hot vacation spots for just the smallest of misdemeanors.

Organized religion is not natural, it is man-made and it is fear based. It is also observable that it has not delivered what it has promised for thousands of years—peace on earth and good will to men.

What Is New Age and New Thought?

New Age and New Thought both consider a direct connection with the creator or "All there Is." Neither belief system endorses organized religious institutes. Sexes are recognized as equal by both groups. Reincarnation is held by both belief systems as the highest display of unconditional love, and is consistent with the idea that we may not experience all that we have to in one incarnation.

Both New Thought and New Age groups are positive and believe in a Loving God, not a vengeful God. Both groups believe that we are all part of God and live within the knowingness that the planet and our society can be transformed.

New Age and New Thought groups both believe that God is life. Where there is life, there is energy. Where there is life, there is consciousness. Where there is consciousness, there is intelligence, where there is Life, there is Light and Love. These attributes are inseparable. They are omnipotent, omnipresent and omniscient—all of them.

Meditation is valued by both structures and is borrowed from Eastern religions. It is the vehicle or the connection between the ego and the spirit within. It's how we communicate with spirit.

New Age and New Thought endorse alternatives to standard orthodox medicine and seek holistic approaches to healing in addition to, or in place of, standard treatment for illness. The power of the mind is favoured in healing practices and is supported by scientific research. New Thought leans more to spiritual healing than does New Age, which uses a broader range of healing that encompasses most all known alternatives, as well as traditional remedies.

Both groups share the same interest in physics and quantum mechanics. Physics supports idealism and is consistent with the fundamental beliefs of "New Age" and "New Thought." New Age can embrace the occult and some of its mystic accoutrements. New Thought does not condemn it, but will discourage interest in it. New Age believes it is possible to practice these alternative beliefs within the framework of Christianity and other religions.

As we move further into the new millennium both New Age and New Thought movements have and will, become increasingly more popular, because traditional churches and organizations have not been able to bring about the positive changes that they promised. New Thought and New Age are consistent with evolutionary trends.

As people become more and more discontented with their environment, and how they live, they will reach out and form new groups and organizations that will accommodate a more progressive philosophy. Since it is only natural that all species generally move in an upward direction or at least a more evolved path, they will begin again to recognize that the separation between the parts is an illusion. We are our brother's keeper and we are joined with the earth, and each other, in a very meaningful and spiritual way.

Both New Thought and New Age groups are flexible and leave space for change and growth. I predict that many of the churches will disappear because of the inflexibility to change to meet the needs of their congregations. The fear that they embrace, is the fear that will facilitate their own downfall. Life is love, and fear is its opposite. Most will be little more than museums in this century if they fail to open up and embrace the new revelations. A closed system has no room for growth.

What Do I Have To "Give Up," To Be Spiritual?

You do not have to give up anything to be spiritual. You are spirit by nature and anything that you do is spiritual.

One of the first things you need to give up to grow spiritually is the notion that there is only one way to the creator. Your way is not the only way, it's just another way. There are an infinite number of ways. Your life is about creating you own path, and you have total freedom to do it anyway you wish.

You are not in the physical world to learn anything and this is not a school. All things are known and are accessible at some level. What you are here to do is experience physical life in all its probabilities. You are life exploring life and the only purpose to your life is that which you give it.

Always keep your mind open for new possibilities, and when you hear something that resembles your truth you will know it, maybe not at first, but it will come to you as a sudden revelation, "the truth just hit me," as an all encompassing knowingness, that you always knew it to be so.

Give up the notion that everybody else is wrong. You cannot judge another because you don't know what they are here to experience. They are entirely correct in their actions, given their model of the world and how they see themselves spiritually. What they are doing in their life now is entirely appropriate for their place in time, in this life's journey.

Do not judge anything around you, but accept that it is the way it is because it is appropriate for it to be so. Know that you have created it personally and collectively with others, and it will change when you all decide that it is no longer appropriate or doesn't work any longer.

Nothing in this world can happen without the complicity of all involved at some level. To say otherwise is to ignore that we are all one and it creates separation. In truth there are no innocent bystanders or victims.

Give up the notion that you cannot change anything that doesn't work for you. You created everything in your life. You also have the power to change it, simply by changing what you thought about it.

Give up the idea that you have to live in misery or poverty. Give up the idea that you were put here to suffer; this is a religious based perception that has no truth in nature. Man was never meant to suffer, he does so at his only bequest.

Give up the idea of heaven or hell. Know that you are already there and it is only your perception of what is. Life has no meaning, save for the meaning that you give it. If you see only angels, you have made it to heaven. If you see only devils, this is your hell. Both exist at the same time and place, here and now. When you know this, you will not choose to be in hell. You will start to see things differently and begin to change your thoughts about where you are. You will call this new place heaven.

Give up being so hard on yourself. Know yourself as who you really are. You are unconditional love, you are free, and you are a loving individual who has absolute freedom to choose otherwise.

Give up the idea of being what other people want you to be. Create your own image about who you are. Move outside of the box.

Give up on the idea that you will die, or that you will become extinct. Know that who you really are still lives. You will never loose the essence of who you are and know that the ego is just an illusion and part of the triune. Remember you are mind, spirit and body.

Give up the notion that you even have to do anything. There is nothing you have to say, do or be in order to get back to the creator. How you experience your sojourn in the world is up to you. You are not a victim of any circumstance; you create all the circumstances of your life.

Your trip is guaranteed, you will not ever be judged as unworthy by the creator, only man will do that. Do not use your faith, belief or prayers to become what you want to be, they are simply tools to focus your thoughts. Know that you are already there and proclaim it as being so. That is the "Great Secret" of success. Know that "I am that I am." Know that you already have it and it will be yours.

Give up any belief that you must get down on your knees to anyone or anything. Know that you are the power and that it comes from nowhere outside of self.

What Is So Great Outside Of the Box?

Once again I must remind you that the only reason you have read this far into this book, is because a small voice inside you is alerting you to the fact that there is something better than what you already have. It is your time to move to the next step. Life is better outside the box, and intuitively you know that. There is no coincidence in reading this book, it is happening for a reason. It is the sign you've been looking for.

New opportunities are at hand for you. Along with moving outside of the box comes new wisdom for you. Wisdom that will enhance your life and make it more meaningful. With this new enlightenment comes new pleasures, and new freedom. Being tapped into the system gives you the power of the system to use at your will and pleasure. At best you are now only using an infinitesimal portion of what is available to you in the universe. The universe has no choice but to give you what you want, it is the law, it is a natural law.

Have you ever wondered why some people seemingly less deserving than you, appear to get ahead? Luck follows them around like a best friend, while others struggle for everything they have and are just getting by. What is it that they are doing that you are not? How is it that they can go through life doing less deserving or even harmful things to others and still be rewarded? It's because they know how the system works and you and others do not! Good fortune and luck doesn't even enter into the equation, luck is simply an observable event that something is working in one's favour.

The universe is blind to good and bad, it doesn't exist in the big picture. It is impartial and its only purpose is to give you what you desire. The possibilities are boundless. There are those that know it; whether they use it for good or evil purposes, they are able to manifest it. They do not limit themselves to what others say they can have; they know they can have it all.

At any time you can tap into those powers and have all that you desire. First you must get out of the box and, secondly, you must know that it is all yours if you so desire   Being out of the box is life, being in the box is slow death and a lifetime of repeating the things in your life that don't work for you. You are destined by your own thought processes to fail or have less than you want.

Your new life outside the box brings a knowingness of why you are here and an experience of physical life in its fullest. Beingness outside the box is a blessing and an adventure into new probabilities.

Joy and happiness are what await you outside the box and, whether you are aware of it or not, just by reading this book you will never experience life in the box the same way.

Awareness brings a new desire to explore and experience all that is available to you. You will never want to go back and you will never be the same.

Given a brand new widget that will make your life easier, would you not want to at least try it and to see if it really does work? Would you be something less than human if you did not? Knowingness brings desire to experience. It is natural for you to want to experience; it is the purpose for which you came. Until you know that, you will not be out of the box.

What Are the Benefits of Being Outside the Box?

❖ Learn how to manifest effectively to give you what you desire.

❖ Learn how to heal yourself and others.

❖ Learn how to control so called natural disasters.

❖ Learn about other civilizations and life forms on other Realms of existence.

❖ Learn about the other senses that you now have, which are latent within your being.

❖ Learn how you can have peace on earth through a collective consciousness that is your own.

❖ Learn how to use the future, to give you new choices and direction.

❖ Learn about your connection with mother earth and all living things on it.

❖ Learn how you project your thoughts into the future so that you can return to the past to make it so.

❖ Learn how to work with the environment for mutual benefit, including controlling the weather.

True spiritual living does not take on any of the formal trappings or posturing of most organized religions, institutions or any weird "spaced out" cults. Spiritual living is simple, as life was meant to be. It's about finding out what works for you and then manifesting it. It's about being yourself. It's about being happy and then going out and doing happy things. It's is about recognizing the symbols in your life that represents what's going on internally. It's about planting seeds that will bring you joy and prosperity. It's not about suffering and doing without. It's about never being sick or having accidents, and it's about having abundance, joy and happiness until you no longer desire to experience it.

Spirituality is about raising your personal vibration level to where you become a beacon in your family, neighbourhood and community. It's not about doing great things, but about being who you are. That is the greatest secret; there is nothing you have to be, but yourself.

There is some quality that only you have that is inimitably yours. It is this quality that makes you special, that brings you here now, at this time. This is your purpose for being here, to manifest a thought process that represents your unique image in a physical environment.

If I told you that you could go to heaven without doing anything special, how would that make you feel? If I told you that you would not be punished by God for anything that you've done, anything, how would that make you feel? If I told you that there was no such place as hell, except in your own thoughts, how would that make you feel?

Is it too much for you to believe that you are absolutely free to experience yourself, how ever you want, and that's the reason for you being here? If I told you that this is what it is like living out of the box, how would you now feel?

Now, how many excuses can you come up with for not believing any of this stuff? How long do you think it is going to take you, to talk your way back into the box? The truth is. it doesn't really matter. If it is your time to be in the box, that is the way it will be and it is entirely appropriate. The only difference now is that you know something that will make a difference. You have choices that you were unaware of before you read this book, and you will without a doubt, want to experience it.

You can never go back to being the same as you were before. You have taken the first step out of the box and you have, once again started your journey. Loosen up and enjoy the trip—you cannot, not get there. It doesn't matter how long it takes you, whether one or a thousand lifetimes, you will return. You have a choice whether you want to be pro-active and conscious in how you go about it or you can be unconscious, it doesn't matter and that's the whole point. IT DOESN'T MATTER!

Chapter 6

Will I Make God Angry?

To say that God gets angry about anything is to assume that He is subject to the same emotions as we are. Our emotional system is human and it was designed to help us survive in the physical world. In order to believe that God gets angry you would have to also say that there is something God cannot have or do. If you believe that, it would make Him a lesser God.

If God is all there is, then God is complete, what is there that He could not have if He so wished? What would there be to be angry about, and if God is subject to human emotion such as anger and vengeance, why the hell are we still here? I would have gotten rid of all the bad guys a long time ago?

To believe that God gets angry is a notion put upon us by organized religion that interpret God in humanity's image. The church has made God a lesser god, in most cases an angry, vengeful god.

In truth, God is emotionless. As with all other things physical and non-physical humans project their emotions onto a god that has no need for emotions. That is not to say that He does not have desires that would be incorrect, purpose is its own desire.

How would seeking another way back to the creator make Him angry? If He was emotional, would He not rejoice? Would the angels not sing, would the heavens not open up to let you in, no matter how you got there?

If we are to believe that the very essence of what God embodies is unconditional love, would it really matter how you got back to God, just as long as you got back? If man could forgive the prodigal son, then God being greater than man, could He not also forgive or is He a lesser god?

The creator doesn't care how you get back, He will celebrate your returning, and you will be glorified at the reunion no matter what path you take. You will not be punished, some the whole event described above is metaphorical. It doesn't happen that way.

Will I Burn In Hell?

Yes, if that is what you believe. Both Heaven and Hell are humanity's concepts of the afterlife. They are manifested symbols of your present thought process. What you believe now is what you will take with you when you die. If you believe there is a hell, then you will experience it after you leave your body. It will be your truth until you realize that you don't have to be there. You will then raise yourself up.

Pope John Paul II stated at the Vatican on July 18, 1999, "Hell is a state of separation from God, a state caused not by a punishing god but rather, self- induced." The biblical descriptions of hell are symbolic and metaphorical.

Will I Loose My Friends?

Walking the road less traveled can be lonely at first, until you start to draw people of like mind to you. As you grow past the understanding of your friends, some of them may reject you, or you may simply drift apart. Your family may consider you just weird but they tolerate you. There will be many of those belonging to organized religions that will label you a heretic and condemn you. You will also feel a parting of the ways. Many people that have been close to you for a long time will begin to make less and less sense to you, as you begin to experience more and more sense.

Common Fears

- ❖ I'm afraid I will be punished by God.
- ❖ My friends will laugh at me and think I'm weird.
- ❖ People will be angry with me.
- ❖ I will be kicked out of my church.
- ❖ I'm afraid of being brainwashed by some weird cult.
- ❖ I am afraid I will be wrong.
- ❖ I am afraid I will not be accepted.

❖ I will not be able to return to my old ways.
❖ I will not be respected.
❖ I will be wasting my time.
❖ I will hurt someone.

Life has no meaning save the meaning you give it. Why not give it a purposeful meaning, your meaning? It is your life and not anybody else's. Does it not make sense to sing your song, create your music and dance your dance? Your life is all about you, it's only you, and you are creating it in each and every moment with every choice that you make. You are always free to live your own life as you chose. It's all about you.

I read about an American solder who was captured during the Vietnam War and was placed in solitary confinement for the time he was a P.O.W. For the seven years that he suffered under the most inhumane conditions, he created a whole new reality in the darkness of his prison cell. He played golf every day. He lived freely on the course and he always played great golf. A round of golf on a full size course can take up to five hours and this is how he spent his time in his cell. He was wise to choose a great game and new friends to experience it with. His captors could not break him. He created a whole new world for himself that was just as real as the one you are experiencing now.

One of the first things he did after his liberation was to play golf. Because he became so good at it in his mind, the first time he played again on a real course he played his best game ever.

Though you may lose some friends along the way, you will create new like-minded friends at every turn along the road to enlightenment. Those friends that love you unconditionally will celebrate your liberation, and you will inspire them to follow.

For those who dare to crawl out of the box and take the road less traveled, the rewards are many. You will become aware of new concepts, heightened senses, new psychic awareness and pleasures you never imagined before. Columbus dared to venture past the edge of the earth and instead of falling off into the abyss, he discovered new lands, peoples and riches and dispelled a world-held truth that the planet was flat.

Will I have to Travel to Tibet to See the Great Buddha?

No one can live your life for you. You are now living it appropriately, given your model of the world and how you see yourself in relationship to your environment. If you don't like the way it is, you simply change your thoughts about it and take the steps that bring about the changes you imagined.

Traveling to Tibet to see the great Buddha will give you some awareness, but the answers that are appropriate for the life you imagined are already within you. That is the place to look, go within. For all those who have gone to Tibet, this is what they will tell you, this is the "Great Secret." I will tell you a Great Buddha story.

A man did go to Tibet to see the Great Buddha and to find the secret to his enlightenment. He spent his whole life searching for the secret, and this was his last resort.

After traveling for days up the Himalayas, and suffering all kinds of hardships including dehydration and hunger, he passed out on the steps of the home of the Great Buddha. The Buddha found him and took him into his room. The man having regained consciousness, asked the Buddha the secret to enlightenment.

Before answering, the Buddha asked the man if he would like a cup of tea, the man replied that he would. As the Buddha poured the tea into the cup the man watched, and observed that the tea was running over the top of the cup. The man mentioned this to the Buddha, and the Buddha replied that this was the answer that he sought, this was the great secret. The man thought about the demonstration, but could not figure it out. After some time elapsed, the Buddha enlightened him.

This is the "Great secret!"

"If you are going to fill your cup with new tea, first you must empty your cup!"

Will This New Enlightenment Get Me into Heaven?

Here is another great secret; you are already where you say you want to be. There is no place you have to go to get to Heaven, Nirvana, The Promised Land, Mecca, Stovokor—if you are Klingon—is all around you. These places are only human concepts. Life after your physical death begins now, and it's here. Whatever your concept of heaven is, that is what you will experience. You create it and you take it with you when you die.

There are people all around you that see only the good in everybody. You see them all the time and wonder how they can be so happy with everything that is going on in the world today. In their daily lives they do not see the ugliness or unhappiness that you witness or experience, they see only the beauty. Their lives are filled with love for themselves, others and the world they live in. How is it possible for them to be here and not see what's going on? How can they not be involved? Surely they must have their heads buried in the sand?

Look around you, see the angels and you will know that you are in heaven. Look around you, see the devil, and you will know hell. Heaven and hell are not places to go to. That's where you already are, it's your present experience. Become aware of this and you will begin to see only angels.

Will I Be Able To Walk Through Walls or Fly?

You must be careful what you think. You live in a dimension of illusion. What you know will be so! If you want to prove that you can fly or walk through walls, then that is what you will get back, a process of proving you can walk through walls and you will fail. If you simply know that you can do it, then there is no need to prove it.

The physical is not really solid. It has the illusion of solidity because of time and space. The distance between you and a rock, for instance, gives you the illusion that the rock is solid. Yet if you get really close to the rock and look at it under a powerful microscope you decrease the distance or space, and you will notice there are spaces between the atoms of the rock. If you get even closer, the spaces become massive distances, as the distances between planets and you would be able to travel between them.

Time and space are part of the illusion so that we may experience the physical plane. There have been many stories through our history of people flying, or walking, through walls. Most of the religious texts refer to people flying or rising up. Theoretically, by changing the vibration of the atoms in your person you will be able to do it.

Be careful of what you judge to be real. Knowingness is not blind faith, wishful thinking or desire. It is the first step in manifesting and is omnipotent and absolute.

Will My Life Improve?

The great secret to improving your life is simply changing your thoughts about it. Stop to smell the flowers and you will begin to know the beauty in the life you already have. Your life is not static, it moves. The great secret to happiness is to be happy first, and then go out and do happy things. We, as a species, have "it" backwards. We believe we have to do things to make us happy. Whatever you want to be, be that first, then begin to demonstrate it symbolically in physical form.

Once you move past the illusion, you'll be able to see the greater picture and find happiness in anything that you do. As in my story about the P.O.W., he played a great game of golf everyday during his incarceration, and for five hours a day he knew happiness. He managed to raise himself to a different level of consciousness that was real for him.

Executioners through our history have observed this phenomenon on some prisoners before their impending death. They have found happiness and serenity, even though they face the termination of their corporal existence, often in a very inhuman fashion.

Your life will always improve when you start believing that it can, and finally know it to be true.

Chapter 7

WYSIWYG

WYSIWYG, or wizzywig, is an acronym. It's a computer term meaning "What You See Is What You Get." WYSIWYG technology allows you to type or create a graphic on you screen and the printer will produce an exact copy on paper.   Imagery is extremely important in manifesting what you want to experience in the physical world. All physical objects are symbols of where you are spiritually. They are manifested thoughts.

We surround ourselves with objects of our desire. These are choices we have made and they clearly show our taste and preferences. They are important in that they remind us of who we are. We collect and save things because they remind us of our history and who we were, they are sign posts or markers.

In the process of manifesting we create an internal image of what we desire. At some level that image starts to solidify. If we keep the image, and focus on it long enough, it will become real. We will begin to experience that image physically at some level of our consciousness. In truth, we project our image into the future then go back into the past to start doing the things that will bring it into our reality.

In conclusion

I will repeat myself again. Nothing matters; life has no meaning save for the meaning you give it. You have nothing to prove and there is nothing you have to do, say or be. Your return to the creator is guaranteed and you will not go to hell unless you believe that you will.

You can go through this life, consciously or unconsciously. You have free will to experience anything in this life without punishment from God. Only man will punish you. Every action you take is appropriate for you, considering your model of the world. Everything you do, or say, is a symbol of where you are on the evolutionary ladder.

Punishment and consequences are not the same. Consequences are what happen to you when you break a law of nature. Punishment is what is put upon you for breaking one of man's laws.

There is no place for you to go, no place to hide and no place to escape to. Because we are all one soul who would you be hiding from? We exist everywhere at the same time. The soul is omnipresent, omniscient and omnipotent.

There are two things that, so far I have identified in my studies that most people will agree on fundamentally. I use these two things as a guide, if what I am reading or being told does not come back to them. I reject the information as not being part of my truth.

"God is unconditional love, God is omniscient, omnipresent and omnipotent!"

There are no innocent victims and at some level all souls must cooperate; all souls must cooperate for a event to happen. Again, nothing can happen to you or anyone else without their complete cooperation at some level of consciousness.

There is only "one" soul. We are all individualized pieces of that one soul, as a wave is to the ocean. We are the parts that make up the whole. We were given free will so that the "one" soul could experience itself in all aspects of itself.

It is my desire that you not make this book, or anyone else's works, your new bible. Use it to inspire you to create your own. Use this book as a stepping stone to something even greater along your path less traveled.

Know always that you can do no wrong. Wrong is a human concept. Know that we are all individualized pieces of God with free will. God does not punish, for whom would there be to punish? Finally, remember the great truth—LIFE HAS NO MEANING EXCEPT THAT WHICH YOU GIVE   IT!

BOOK TWO

The Power of Healing

Introduction

The first series of books I have written are very basic and I hope to attract people that are just starting out. I have left out some detail and tried to make the writing very much uncomplicated. Should something I have written peak your interest I would hope you would read some of the other more comprehensive books on the subject. You will find them listed in the back of this book.

I would like to believe that those that have become aware would know that there is more to themselves than the body, and are willing to open themselves up to new possibilities outside the box, and become an expert on spirituality. They may not be able to express it, but they have a knowingness that is authentic.

Having a PhD, or being part of an organized belief system, has many drawbacks to teaching authentic spirituality. The truth about who you are is internal and changing, and you will find your truth within. There is no formal training for being a true spiritualist—you simple are one.

Doctors, psychologists, psychiatrists and clergy often write books that include many biases as packaged truth. Some of the things they write represent worn out clichés and metaphoric religious dogma. Their training often gets in the way of expressing what they know intuitively. They will side with established tradition, and take the easy or safe way out.

True spirituality goes beyond the safe zone and often puts the writer at risk. They cannot afford to let their true spirituality shine through their degrees, it just sounds like it does. At this point I must say there certainly are some very gifted professional people. With a little practice and awareness you will recognize them.

The first stories in this book will give you some insight into my early beginnings, and the family that I grew up around. All of us have an illness of some kind whether it be physical or psychological, it just may not have been discovered yet, or have a label attached to it.

As with many families, mine was dysfunctional. We lived in poverty without a father figure. From my vantage point I was able to see the dysfunction, and I found a way to survive.

From ignorance, I lived most of the rest of my life, allowing my past to guide my present and future. I allowed those early circumstances to colour my present thoughts about how I would live my life. My story will demonstrate that to you.

My sister and brother's stories will also give you insight into how we carry over familiar behavioural situations into our present circumstances. The sad part of it is we do it from choice, freedom of choice, and it is so unnecessary. We may escape the prison, but we often bring the chains with us.

When I read this book for the first time after I had printed it, it was like seeing it for the first time. I cannot take credit for some of the writing, as I believe the message came through me and not from me. You may recognize some of it as being your story.

I do know that any kind of spiritual enlightenment does not come from a degree. You are qualified the moment you realize there is something more than what you know as *yourself* and you start moving toward it. The more degrees you have, or the more you try to explain it in human terms, the farther you move away from your truth. Spiritualism or spirituality is simply knowingness and this is what makes you, or anyone, an expert on the subject. It is a process and we all process differently.

As my books and essays continue to make less sense to me, I recognize that I am still moving to another level of understanding, I am moving farther along the path I have chosen and I am still experiencing my awareness. I do not want to stop at being an expert, nor do I want to pretend to be one. I am simply here to experience

The purpose of my book is not to give you a quick fix or lessons on how to live your life. It is simply to bring awareness into your life, though it is mine, perhaps you will benefit from it.

Spirituality "101" is not a means to an end. In fact, it has no meaning at all if you cannot experience it, and you do not want to miss the opportunity of a lifetime. Higher learning means nothing if you cannot apply it, or have gained no wisdom from the experience.

I am very proud of this book, and the other material that I have written. I hope they will have a great impact in the lives of the people who read them.

I cannot give meaning to this book, only you can do that.

This book is not about false hope or faith, it's about understanding a process. That is what you are, you are in the process of living and creating everything in your life, including your own health and well-being.

Enjoy the book, loosen up a bit, open your mind to new possibilities, and then write your own book.

When you have finished this book, you will know why you are sick, why you are not healed yet, and why you have accidents. You will know the "great secret," to staying well so that there is no need to be healed. You will know how to heal others, and stay away from accidents.

BOOK TWO

Chapter 1

People I Meet That Are Sick

With more than 30 years in the service industry I have been in thousands of homes, and have been able to interact with people one on one, and see how they live. I have met all kinds of people, mostly healthy people, and some in various conditions of ill health. A couple of these people have stuck out in my mind and I want to share their stories with you.

A recent visit with an older person stirred me the most. I met this man's wife at the door, and we walked around the house, while I did my inspection. The house was a large, modernly designed home, less than ten years old. The yard was beautifully kept and landscaped. The owners had spared no expense in keeping up the house and surrounded themselves, lavishly, with expensive furniture and fixtures.

When I had finished the inspection, the lady invited me to talk to her husband at the kitchen table. A distinguished grey haired man was sitting, hunched over the table, as I walked into the room. He spoke to me in a heavy Italian accent. I sat with him and talked for a while.

I learned that he had come to Canada as a younger man and made his fortune here. His kids were grown and had scattered themselves around the country. He also let me know that he was getting ready to go to mass. He goes to church every day to pray for his healing. He told me he was dying of cancer. For months he had been praying to God to release him of his sickness. The situation seemed hopeless, and his voice had a slight sound of bitterness to it. I felt an unusual sense of compassion for this man. He was talking from his physical consciousness and as he was doing so, I could see the beauty in his story from a different perspective—not clouded by his pain.

I handed him a crystal that I had in my pocket. I keep it there to remind myself at all times that I am well, and I have power over my health. I gave it to him to hold in his hand and told him a brief story about it. The expression on his face remains with me today while I watched the man clutch the crystal as a drowning man to a life preserver. I wished I had given it to him. He seemed to draw some comfort from it and, at that point, in his life, he was ready to grab onto anything that would give him hope. His money was totally worthless to him and he knew it.

The memory of this man has remained in my mind for some reason. Possibly because I have imagined him as a strong man in his day, with lots of power and money, but now wasted away to a portion of what he was, and ready to grab at any straw to hold onto the last bit of his life. His religion so far had failed him. His God was ignoring him, and he had nowhere to turn. *The great secret* had evaded him in the last days of his life, and he had been so close to knowing the truth all his life. I felt helpless at the time to tell him anything that might comfort him. His situation had been a long process and I am sure he had heard it all. I believe that he had finally accepted the inevitability of his death but was still going through the motions of hanging onto hope and faith, for the sake of his wife.

A School Mate

For most of my working career I worked as an electronics technician in a small shop in my hometown. During my tenure with this company I got to know some of the customers very well. One character especially sticks out in my mind. Reg was a funny person, a little crude and rough around the edges, but very good-hearted and I believe, one of the smartest people I know. He was very active and could not sit still for very long, ever productive and a marvellous inventor. He always had a project going, sometimes to the dismay of his family.

I never really got to know him that well, until I quit the job and started my own business. The man became one of my most admired friends and a great customer of mine.

His kids grew up and moved away from home and he eventually separated from his one and only wife. Reg bought a small house on acreage and outfitted his garage to do mechanical repairs for the locals.

He talked often about the projects he wanted to complete before he died. Prospecting for gold and building a small hydroponics shed in his back yard were his future pet projects. Reg loved to fish and always had a boat or two in his yard that were in the process of restoration. He would fix them up to his liking only to sell them, and buy another to repeat the process.

Reg saved some money and had a very small mortgage on his house. He was financially secure but insisted on being productive. He repaired things, bought equipment, rebuilt it and sold it. This man never had enough time for prospecting, or building his hydroponics. He seldom made time for his most loved projects. The more available he was the more people would call on him. He was honest and reliable. Reg is in his seventies and the long hours were starting to show on him. He began to complain about being taken advantage of, and working too hard. He wanted rest, he wanted to get away and prospect for gold. Prospecting was something that he had done before and it was not just a pipe dream.

My good friend finally found a way to get the time to do the things he really wanted to do. He had a stroke, which left him paralyzed down his left side. Part of his good life was smoking and drinking heavily and it finally caught up with him. Because he could not make the decision to take life easy himself, life did it for him.

This is not the end to this story. Reg loves life and there was never enough time to do all the things that he wanted to do. He went into physiotherapy. He learned how to walk again and his speech came back. He has almost fully recovered in just over two years.

Reg is still involved in his projects, but now only for himself. He takes his time and is not in a hurry. He has learned to enjoy the gifts that have been given to him for his own enjoyment. He has learned how to take care of himself and he expects to be around for some time to come. He is unable to go prospecting, but he still putters around in his garage. I do not know if he knows about the "Great Secret," but he certainly learned how to use it.

There Were Four of Us

As children, my two siblings and I were kept away from people who were sick. Even when our pets got sick we were not allowed to be with them. Many times the sick people or animals died, and we missed spending time with them. We were spared their suffering or any special moments to talk to them.

Today it is very difficult for me to empathize with people who are ill, and I regret that. I have never had a model for compassion and often felt alienated from people that did. I believe that one of the best ways to learn empathy is to be involved with or allowed to experience the symptoms of others' sickness or grief. It is a wonderful opportunity to be in touch with the spiritual side of people. It would seem that most people who are sick have let down their guards, and have allowed themselves to be closer to their spiritual sides during moments of great despair.

My mother used to say that their sickness was all in their heads. She would also say that about us, when we had minor ailments. She did not really know how close to the truth she was. I grew up thinking some of the same things. The sins of the Mother are passed on to her children. When one of us, or one of our friends, got sick we would accuse them of faking it and offer no sympathy.

My mother was incorrect in not letting us empathize with sick people, or be there for them. She was correct, however, in saying that it was all in their heads and she was very close to the "Great Secret."

Tragically, she did not get the attention she wanted when she got sick. Finally, when she died of a heart attack, there was no one there for her. Her children were left with her legacy of indifference and never attended her funeral.

When the children of my first marriage got sick, I down played the experience as much as possible so that they did not dwell upon their illness. I did this from a learned response and ignorance. Later on in the book you will learn why this was the correct thing to do. The difference is that I did not do it from empathy, or in a very loving way.

During the short time I spent with my second family I had mellowed out somewhat, and was slightly more empathetic to my stepchildren when they were sick. Looking back, I was on the road to experiencing empathy and compassion but I still did not know the *Great Secret.*

My Sister

At this point I want to make the reader aware that during my childhood our mother raised my siblings and I, on her own, in dire poverty. There were times when all we had for supper was bread fried in grease.

As children living in boxed poverty, we did not dwell on it too much. It was normal for us and we expected nothing else. One of the nice things about being in the country back in those days was that we were somewhat insulated or isolated from neighbours. Farm people traditionally are often considered poor. It was only after we started going to school that we really discovered the differences.

My sister was younger than me by one year and my brother older by nearly three years. My father had died of a logging accident some time after my sister was born. We survived on a small pension cheque that my mother received each month, and handouts from family members, and good people in the community.

Needless to say, my early life would appear to have been difficult. We were always at odds with each other and would be fighting constantly. My brother would pick on me, and I would pass it down to my sister. My mother would equalize the whole affair by punishing all of us.

As we grew older the family became more dysfunctional, each of us finding our own special way of surviving, including my mother.

My brother became a bully. He was always in trouble at school and in the neighbourhood. He picked on us showing no mercy and he was always beating on us. He became such a trouble maker that my mother had to side with him against my sister and I, to help calm down the situation.

I withdrew and became reclusive. I found that if I was quiet and disappeared I could avoid most of the trouble in the household. I found my own secret hiding places and made friends with myself. I could easy sneak around the house without anyone seeing or hearing me.

Today I still have reclusive tendencies and manifest that in my everyday life. On a conscious level I try to make myself available and open, but have not fully recovered from this sickness, a dysfunction that I have not come to terms with fully.

My sister found her own special way of getting attention and staying out of trouble. She would become ill. When things did not go her way or she was being ignored or picked on, she would develop some kind of illness. When I look back at this little girl, I feel so much empathy towards her now. She was at the bottom of the pecking order and took the worst of it. Both my brother and I would blame things on her in order to avoid the wrath of our mother. I remember how relieved and guilty I felt that it was her being punished, not me.

My brother and sister are opposites and never have been very close. They have distanced themselves and it would not be safe to leave them alone in a room together, even today. None of us for that matter, communicates with each other very well. No healing between us has occurred after all these years and time has not healed any of the wounds. I seldom see either, and neither of them talk to each other.

My sister's illnesses were certainly real to her and all of us around her. She was rushed to the hospital many times with serious symptoms. There she received the attention she craved and was immune from local punishment.

Vomiting was not a good thing to do in our household. I remember my sister and I being punished for it. We received no special consideration for such an action. Getting sick was a huge inconvenience and expense for my mother. We simply could not afford to get sick.

As an adult, my sister's illnesses were very profound and life threatening. She has had every kind of cancer you can think of, and numerous heart attacks. This is somewhat exaggerated, but I have lost track of what she has been in the hospital for. She has had most all the ailments that are listed in the medical books. My sister's survival techniques are well honed and still serve her well. She is well aware of her hypochondriac tendencies and is now controlling them with professional help. Psychologically, she has come along way, but her memories of her childhood remain distorted and dysfunctional.

My sister is very artistic and finds some relief in drawing and publishing children's books. She has received a measure of success with her art and I know that this has allowed some healing in her life. Still I am unaware of her becoming aware of the *Great Secret.*

My mother's dysfunction was apparent when she did not get her way. She would try to manipulate us with her tears and guilt and I regret not being able to empathize with or comfort her. I did not know which tears were genuine, or what I could do to help when she needed comforting. Mother taught us that the tears could not be trusted. After years of avoiding tears, I have come to realize that it is OK to cry, and comfort people who are crying.

Mind Over Illness

My grandmother had an accident and walked with a limp. From time to time, as a youngster, I would mimic her limp and I thought it was funny. This was always good for getting a measure of attention from my brother or sister. Grandma would grumble a bit and shrug it off.

A short time before I started my first year in grade school my limping appeared on its own. From time to time, my hip would hurt and I would complain to my mother. She thought I was still making fun of my grandmother. This went on for a time and, although I do not remember the event, an appointment with the doctor ensued. I never thought any more of it and soon forgot.

One day after only a short time in my first month of grade school, my grandmother arrived at my school and took me home for the day. My mother explained that, in fact there was something wrong with my hip. The doctors did not know what it was, but they wanted me in the hospital for examination.

It is ironic that the family was going through some trying times. Even though I had found a way to separate myself from the family most of the time, I managed to find an even better way and distance myself further. As a young boy of only five or six years, I managed the will at some level of consciousness to remove myself from a bad situation.

The doctors admitted me into the Royal Columbian Hospital where I underwent examinations. All the tests were inconclusive and the local doctors did not know what the ailment was. They narrowed it down to one of two possibilities, either polio or perthes disease. After several weeks of lying in bed and sometimes in traction, I received the news that I was going to be transferred to the Shriners Hospital for Crippled Children in Spokan, Washington.

For all the fuss that occurred I still did not understand the circumstances of my ailment. I could still walk and most of the time it did not hurt, but they would not let me out of bed. When they were not looking I kept trying my legs out and they were fine. I could walk without any pain or limp. This hospital stuff was a great inconvenience for me. The only thing I knew was that I could still walk.

At the time, the local treatment for Perthes was to cut a section of bone out of the hip. This would leave me with a permanent limp. I was truly blessed at this time by being transferred to the US hospital. The doctors decided to do nothing except put me in a cast so I would not walk around, and they demanded complete bed rest.

Retrospectively, I can see that I manifested the perfect escape. I was in no danger from anyone at home, and there would be no operation, the disease was temporary and I would be back on my feet in just over a year, completely healed and declared a miracle child. I was the first ever to be treated in this fashion, and fully recover. I have told very few people this story and I have always considered it a part of my past and just plain history. The incident has not really had any significant meaning to me on a conscious level, until now.

Now I call can tell you because the story will have some benefit for you.

By following my story you can see how I manifested the events of my life. I created the illness that led me to safety, and then I created the cure that took me out of danger from the disease. Circumstances that sometimes seem to be less favourable will often lead to something better, like taking a detour and discovering a new town, or a new restaurant, or running into someone who will have meaning in your future, or what have you. All circumstance has meaning and endless possibilities. Sickness is not always for the worse.

At that time of my life, I only knew intuitively about the "*Great Secret.*" I was not to learn about it until I was much older, at 52 years of age. Now I know, and now I want to pass it on to you.

Chapter 2

Why Do People Get Sick?

Most doctors today will tell you frankly that about 85% of all illnesses are psychosomatic. They are created by us, in our heads. And much of the remaining 15% may be prevented. We all create our own illnesses. The body already has these illnesses that lay dormant within us and it is our own thoughts that activate them. You don't have to go anywhere to catch a cold from somebody else. You just have to activate it, and it's already there. Behind every illness there is a thought that triggers it, a root cause for the illness. Illness has reason for being, and behind illness is an intelligence.

Have you ever noticed, for instance, that the day before and the day after a stat holiday there are a many people getting sick? Now we know for the most part, that these people are saying they are sick so they can get another day or two off. However, whether it's actually them being sick or their bosses experiencing them being sick, they are not at work because they are sick. The whole purpose of the lie is to create the illusion of sickness as a means to an end. Many of these people will get sick during their holidays because of their thoughts; it is an error in thinking.

Herein lays a clue to the "Great Secret" about health and healing.

> "Illness is often the result of dissociated and inhibited emotions."—*Jane Roberts, "The Seth Material."*

As you may recall, my sister got sick in order to get attention or escape punishment. Many of us will go to great lengths to get sick, or have accidents so that we call attention to ourselves. Right now our medical plan is over-burdened by many older people who are looking for attention. They are not really physically sick, and yet the act of pretending to be sick is an illness in itself. They are sick of not being noticed.

People who are very lonely find that illness often brings them the attention they would not otherwise receive. As a species we are social by nature, we crave social interaction, and we will do almost anything to get the recognition.

Attempted suicide is extreme and works very well for those who are seeking attention. Some people have tried numerous times and have never succeeded, only because they don't really want to die. There is absolutely nothing that can stop anyone from killing themselves, if that is what they really want. They have a statement to make and this is how they go about it. They are sick of being ill, or of being lonely. They have not learned the "Great Secret." They don't have to be lonely and they don't have to be sick.

People who are under a lot of pressure at work, or in other surroundings, will become sick to unburden themselves from responsibility, or from the feeling of being overwhelmed or unappreciated.

In some companies sickness is almost epidemic, while other companies enjoy an atmosphere of good health.

In high school I had a classmate who was very popular. He always had lots of friends hanging around him, but when he was put to the test on the soccer or baseball field, and he could see that he might not be able to compete, he would fake an injury. He would get a sprained ankle, or something on the field. The kids would gather around him and give him all sorts of sympathy.

The cause of sickness, whether it is a common cold or a terminal illness, comes from fear. Fear is the opposite of love, and as we move farther away from love we invariably *will* become sick. It is now the number one escape mechanism in our society. We are sick of our job, sick of our mate, sick of our government or sick of the condition of the world. We openly use the word "sick," to describe our feelings about our surroundings and the people we are interacting with, or things that do not work for us anymore. Understanding how we use the word is halfway to knowing the "Great Secret." We use the word automatically without even being aware of it.

I had an opportunity to overhear part of a conversation between two women who were in a heated discussion about something that was going on. One lady turned to the other and declared that she was just "sick" about it and the other confirmed her feelings as well. They both had talked themselves into being sick about an event that was not under their control. They went on to talk about a person that just made them sick, and how there were a lot of sick people in the world. I was getting sick just listening to the conversation.

There are those that are thinking at this moment that saying "you are sick" about a thing is just an expression. They're not really sick, they are just expressing anger. Of course you are correct in this observation, and you would have hit on a key function of manifesting illness if you look a little further. We will touch on that later in the book.

> "He or she, who believes that matter is real of itself, that sickness and disease are realities, or that man has being separate and apart from Spirit, is dwelling in a consciousness of error, a consciousness of darkness."—*Robert Clark*, *"The Christ Mind."*

Worry

One of the most used expressions you hear almost everyday is, "I'm just worried sick about this or that."

Has anyone every worried themselves into sickness? I'm sure we all can relate stories about a mother who has worried herself sick because of the disappearance or illness of a child, or persons that have worried themselves into illness because they could not pay their bills or meet their obligations. What about a spouse who is worried sick about the welfare of the other. They will sometimes worry themselves into a position of being even sicker than the spouse, and some may even die from worry.

If you substitute the word "worry" for "fear," you will begin to understand that when you move away from love you move into realm of *fear* or worry which is the opposite of love.

Love is the understanding that all things are perfect, as it was created by you or in cooperation with another, and nothing happens by chance, luck or lack thereof. Everything that you *fear* or *worry* about was created by you at some level, and is the manifestation of a thought you had about something. I will explain later in the book.

Worry, hate and fear attack the body at the cellular level. It is impossible to have a healthy body under these conditions.

Worry is the emotional equivalent of the fear you have about not getting what you want. I am worried about not being able to pay my bills or, put another way, I fear that I will not be able to meet my financial obligations. I am worried sick that my child will not get well. This equates to, "I am fearful that my child will not get well and I want a healthy child." If your child is already sick then worry is not going to help. Now is the time to think about wellness and about having a perfectly well child. This is another hint as to the "Great Secret," of wellness.

I was a great worrier and I followed in my mother's footsteps. I worried needlessly about everything. When I moved out on my own I started worrying, days in advance, that a payment may not reach a creditor in time. My old car was in better shape than a lot of newer ones. I checked all the lights and signals daily before I took the car out. I worried about the oil and filled my tank when it got half way down. All T's had to be crossed and all I's dotted. Today I'm still always on time and for the most part early.

I cannot say that I worried myself sick. There has been little outward evidence of that. In fact I am perfectly healthy and always have been for the most part. On other hand I did lose lots of sleep. Worry kept me awake for hours after I went to bed and I would lie awake worrying about something. I grew up in the sixties and seventies and it is absolutely a miracle that I did not turn to drugs for some relief from worry.

The sickness that I now face is one of low self esteem. I bought into the reality that my mother set up for me, and that was one of "giving up." I moved from one interest to another, as most children do. She judged that to mean, I couldn't stick with anything. She was incorrect. I had many interests, but mostly I was looking for escape. When I couldn't find it I would move onto something else, not to mention that sometimes we didn't have the money available for me to move forward on any interest I may have had.

Low Self Esteem

Low self esteem is yet another phrase for fear. You may fear that you do not look attractive enough; you may fear that you are not smart enough to land a good job. You may be apprehensive about your background limiting your opportunities. All of these things are fear-based and we call it low self esteem. Because we do not love ourselves enough we usually sabotage any good opportunity that comes along, because we have a belief system that tells us we are not good enough or deserving. In the absence of self love, there is low self esteem.

In the absence of that which tells us we can have or do anything that we want, we do not recognize the opportunities. In fact, we turn away from them, even though they are staring us in the face, because we may feel undeserving or inadequate.

Love tells us we can fly. Fear stops us from trying and low self esteem kills the opportunity. Love tells us that we are great, fear denies it and low self esteem makes us subservient to greatness. Love tells us we can, fear says we can't, and low self esteem won't even let us try.

"Creativity flourishes with self-esteem and self-confidence."—*Henry Reid, "Edgar Cayce: Channeling Your Higher Self."*

People with low self esteem often use the vehicle of illness to reaffirm their lack of self love, while drugs and alcohol play a major role in the lives of many other people to help ease the pain, and the burden of the load that they carry. Young people may use music and sex to escape a reality they are having problems copying with. Television is the number one addiction in the world today, for the most part, not very beneficial. Watching television robs us of our identity and our imagination, and is a major contributor to our dysfunctional society.

We use television to escape our own reality, and to try to forget about how miserable our lives may be. We are presented with images that re-affirm that we are, in fact a lesser person because we don't have the products that are presented on screen, or a models' body, or a six figure income.

Everywhere we turn there are people and images telling us that we are not beautiful, we do not deserve, and we are not successful. It is hard to imagine anyone that does not have some kind of phobia. At some level we must all feel inadequate, and that creates illness and dysfunction

I will tell you from personal experience that we surrender a little more each day and submit to this belief. We will openly admit that we are less because it is what everyone expects from us. There are a lot of people around us that are eager to help us with that image. Most of the time we fall for the illusion. There are just as many people keen to help us out of our situation, for a wheelbarrow full of gold, rubles and diamonds.

Those in power often view a sick society as a manageable society, dependent and exploitable. A society that is reliant on drugs, welfare and Medicare is one that is going to keep you in business or in office.

I have been a victim of this negative image for a long time and have only recently learned the "Great Secret," that I will reveal shortly.

Playing the Victim

I always get sick. If anybody in the neighbourhood has a cold I will get it!

Have you ever heard that one? If this isn't setting yourself up for illness, I know of no other statement that will do it better. If you want to see what a great manifestor you are, keep repeating that line. I have heard sympathetic spouses say things like that many times. Sympathy pains are very real to the person who is having them. Ask a husband about menstrual cramps and pains associated with pregnancy. Some husbands experience varying degrees of the spouse's pain.

A twin who lives apart, and perhaps hundreds of miles away, may experience the same illnesses as the other twin. Why? This involves very specialized communication and is done at the sub-molecular level. It clearly shows how we are connected, and how we manifest illness, I will touch on that later.

An employee came to me one day and said that he had a terrible toothache. He didn't get much sleep the night before, and he didn't think he would be able to work at the job today. He told all his co-workers about it as well, and received lots of sympathy. I put him to work, and told him not to try too hard but do the best he could. I walked by him many times that morning without saying a thing. He seemed to be fine and had a smile on his face. I was quite sure that he had recovered and was feeling better.

Just before lunch a co-worker walked by and asked him how his toothache was. That was all it took to bring back the pain. He had forgotten all about it and when he got involved in his work he became focused on something other than his pain. For awhile until reminded, he did not experience the toothache. Pain is experienced at a conscious level and that is why they knock you out before surgery.

Hereditary Ailments

Even though doctors admit that most ailments start in your head, this brings forth the question of hereditary diseases. A newborn child coming into this world with a disease does not have a chance to manifest the ailment in the same way we do. How do we explain a congenital heart disease that has plagued the family tree for generations, or cancer, or a respiratory problem?

We all know, or are aware of people who have sickness or medical conditions that they were born with. It doesn't seem fair that these people would start off on the wrong foot, so to speak. Why don't they start off living healthy for a period of time, then go out into the world and get sick through reckless living, poor maintenance or exposure, the way the rest of us do? Why is it that they are born into illness, innocently?

I will explain later why there are no innocent victims, and how this can happen. Looking at the bigger picture you will be able to see the beauty in this illusion. Nothing happens by chance and nobody gets sick by accident.

Disease by Natural Transmission

A great many diseases, of course, are transmitted to us naturally from our interaction with the environment and the people around us. Every day, the probability of us catching some disease is continuous. Some of us never catch anything, and yet the chances of that happening is like standing in the rain and not being hit by a drop. Why do some people walk through endless possibilities of *contracting* illness and never be touched?

As I write this book the world has been awakened to the awareness of West Nile virus and an up-and-coming pandemic that may prove to be the plague of the 21st century. We have not come to terms with aids, and other current diseases, and another one has been unleashed upon us. Who will **contract** it and why? It is part of the "Great Secret," and have you figured it out yet?

"In illness you will find your true being."—*Neale Donald Walsch, "Communion With God."*

I owned a retail business for 16 years. I worked at the business seven days a week for most of those years and I was in contact with thousands of people. Some people came into the store with obvious ailments. They breathed on me, they touched, me and yet I never got sick.

One day an insurance salesman came into my store and tried to sell me a sickness policy. I told him I didn't need any sickness insurance and he asked me why. I told him I was a business owner and I couldn't get sick. I had no time for sickness. Nevertheless, I bought the policy anyways and he later sold me an accident policy as well. In all those years I never used either policy. I was a business owner and I couldn't get sick. This does not apply to many employees. They are guided by a different agenda or thought process.

Chapter 3

The Mechanics of Illness

Our bodies were designed to last forever. We have built into each of us a local pharmacy that produces everything that we need to be healthy, and maintain the status quo. We were never meant to get sick. Because we are individualized pieces of the creator, we have all the attributes and characteristics of the creator. We start our sojourn in this life with the potential to live forever in perfect health.

Our bodies are replaced on an ongoing basis, moment by moment, endlessly. In fact the body is 98% replaced in the first year. Your skin is replaced every four weeks. You get a new liver every six weeks, a stomach lining every five days, a new brain within one year and a new skeleton every twelve weeks. By the time I finish this paragraph I will not be the same person I was when I started it.

Having said this it begs the question. If I basically get a new body every year, why do I still have heart trouble? Why do you still have that limp? Why does someone else still have a respiratory ailment in this so called new body?

I will give you the secret now. Every day we basically do only two things; we create or we remember. It is estimated that we have nearly 65,000 different thoughts everyday. Of all these thoughts 85% of them are the same thoughts we had yesterday, and the day before that, and so on. We are constantly rehashing old news and worthless information.

Our body's functions are given over to subconscious memory to run automatically. Higher functions are done at a conscious level. When we do repetitive things we are acting from memory. When we do something new we are both creating and remembering. We remind the body every second of the day that we have a sickness or an ailment or other physical disability. That is automatically encoded into our DNA, so when the body is renewing itself, it is also reading these encoded messages about the condition of our old body from memory, and faithfully incorporating them into the body as it rebuilds it

We create our own illness, and we also remind ourselves constantly that we have it. We solicit our friends and family to help us. They ask us, "how are you feeling today, how's your back, is your tooth still bothering you, how's your headache?" By doing so they are unintentionally reminding us that we are sick. While the body is trying to renew itself we are constantly telling it that it is sick. Have you every had a headache and forgotten about it, only to have someone remind you by asking, "how is you headache?"   Once again, you're conscious of the pain.

> We reap what we sow, and our thoughts are manifested into reality. What we think we create, what we know is so.

There is only one manifestation of continued fear; that is sickness and illness is an error in thinking. You must know that any belief in sickness, disease, or imperfection is an illusion; you have made it up, you have created it. We live in a world of cause and effect (karma). Illness is the effect created by cause. Cause is always present in consciousness. Change the cause and you change the effect. If the cause is erroneous thinking about being imperfect, the effect will be illness. Know that perfection is what you are embodied, and the effect will be perfection. An effect cannot exist without a cause.

Any manifestation of disease, or sickness is error manifesting in physical form. When you see sickness or disease manifesting, know that you are looking at an error in consciousness, manifesting. You body is a mirrored image of what is going on in your mind.

> "Health and sickness are largely externalizations of our dominant mental and spiritual states."—
> Ernest Holmes, "The Science of Mind."

It follows then that if we can make ourselves sick, we can also make ourselves well. It sounds like some kind of lofty, uncaring or arrogant idea for me to say that your sickness is an illusion— while you are sitting there with a terminal disease and reading this. Please have patience. I respect your decision to read this book and I know that your higher power directed you to it, or you wouldn't be reading it now. There is a reason, although you may not know what it is now.

Understand that all things, good or bad, come from knowingness, not belief. It is not a matter of having faith or wishful thinking, desire or want. It is not a matter of whether you feel you deserve it or not, whether you consider yourself good or bad. At a spiritual level, it is all about what you know to be true for you. You are born from perfection and it is your thoughts that say otherwise. I am talking to you from a higher spiritual level that is not of the body. Your body is just a vehicle for the soul to experience itself in the physical realm.

You are a three part being—mind, body, and spirit. If you do not allow yourself to move your focus from that of the body, none of this will make sense to you. The fact that you are reading this book now says that you are on a new path. Continue on.

What I am telling you now comes from my own personal experience, as well as those of others. It is my truth, it doesn't have to be yours. In fact, I would hope that this book would lead you to something that is more evolved, more intuitive. I want you to create your own new truth, and one that knows that you are perfectly healthy.

For all the reasons, and more, as mentioned in chapter two, you create erroneous thinking that leads to sickness and ill health. At some stage you are thinking sick, and then eventually you get sick. The "Great Secret" to not getting sick is to not think sick at any level. Constantly monitor your thoughts. Watch your lifestyle, and all those subtle thoughts of imperfection that creep up in your thinking.

When you don't maintain your body and keep it in harmony with your spirit you will get sick. Poor diet, lack of sleep and exercise are indicators of a poor thought process that leads to illness. Dysfunctional relationships—business, personal or otherwise—are indicators of a poorly functioning thought process and that will lead to sickness. A high level of emotional baggage is another indicator of a poor thought process that will lead to illness.

If you find yourself being drawn to places and people that are already sick, this should tell you something about how you are thinking. If you are sitting with people that dwell on operations, sickness and death, get out fast. If you are taking unnecessary risks at work, home, on the road or elsewhere then there is something that you are doing that is not working for you, and your thinking is erroneous. You have wondered off the path that leads to wholeness.

Move away from your ego and back to your senses. They tell you your truth. The ego tries to reason your feelings and often fails you, so trust your intuition. Your feelings are your truth, they reflect your soul's purpose. Ego's thoughts are based on old truths; your true feelings are based on new truths, and when reacted on produce or demonstrate your new thought   process.

BOOK TWO

Chapter 4

Why Do We Want to Get Well?

"A spiritual approach to healing acknowledges not only that God is the Source of all healing, but also that all healing comes through the Spirit from within our one inner being. Thus, healing is not the result of merely external application or internal medication, but rather of attuning to the Spirit within. The term spiritual implies a constellation of considerations, including purpose, intent, desire, motivation, and ideals."—*Herbert B. Puryear, "The Edgar Cayce Primer."*

I have found a reasonable explanation to the question that is most always asked, "Why are some people healed and others aren't?"

The purpose for which one wants to be healed is of the utmost importance, and is the "Great Secret." Why do you want to be healed—so that you can go back to the same life style that led to the illness? As a matter of fact most of us want to be healed for just that reason—so that we may return to our previous life patterns.

I believe that there are only two good reasons why we should want to be healed. The first is our desire to change—that is changing the patterns that led to the illness—and the second is our desire to serve ourselves and others better.

Spiritual healing begins then as we reorient our desire, purposes, and ideals toward being one with, and a conduit for, the flow of the Spirit.

What would be the point of being healed if we returned to the thinking that made us ill or injured in the first place? Would we not simply manifest the same affliction again? Healing begins within. First we must find out the root cause of the thinking that caused the illness or injury and then vow to replace that thinking. Remember cause and effect—Karma!

If desire for health leads instead to an emphasis upon symptoms to be overcome, you would be better off to avoid all thoughts of health or illness. Such thoughts can lead to focusing on different elements that stand in the way of healing. This just adds energy to the realization of illness.

Sickness and injury are an outward manifestation of what is going on inside us, and the sickness is the result. People that never get well or are chronically sick, have not learned this "Great Secret." The best healing is not to get sick or injured in the first place. Stay attuned to the spirit—stay well!

The way we were raised, and the conditions that we went through as children, are not reasonable excuses for the way we live now. As mature adults we have choices. How we live is always ours to decide, within the boundaries we have set for ourselves. Whether we are free or held prisoner by another, the truth will set you free. Know that you created it, and you will be set free.

I refer back to the reason why my sister had ongoing health problems. For her being ill was a safe haven. Because it became a pattern in her earlier life, she carried it over into her adulthood. She will never get sick again when she discovers that she is in complete control of her life and manifests everything in it. She is not a victim of circumstances, she is creating them. When she learns to create only good things in her life, she will not imprison herself within the confines of sickness, and she will be free because she will know that she created it all. She will know the root cause of her illness and will not go back there.

My brother, the "*authoritarian one*" amongst the siblings, has never healed himself. He only understands dominance and force, and that has led him into trouble most of his life. He did not align himself with people of good character, and was used by most of them. In his sickness he has known only violence, always looking to be loved and acknowledged. The "Great Secret" eluded him as well.

My brother has not learned what the thinking was behind his actions and choices, and as my mother did all her life, he blamed others for his misfortune as well. To him, I would say look inside, love yourself and forgive yourself first, and you will then find the desire to be healed. In retrospect, and even somewhat today, I was always afraid of authority figures. I believed that if I was perfect, invisible, and didn't get into trouble people would leave me alone. I did not realize that I had any power at all, and I never learned to love myself.

There was no way I could get well and overcome disempowerment, until I understood that I had control over whom and what I created in my life. Even at that young age I had the power to love myself, and make the choice to survive, and to allow myself to be loved by others. Learning the "Great Secret" has taken all my life. Only now, at age 55, can I claim my healing, The root cause of my illness no longer escapes me.

None of us kids had any authority over our lives; it was taken away from us at an early age. It has only come back with a higher understanding of who I am. I am now able to claim what was always inherently mine; love, freedom, power and purpose.

There are those that would say I had no choice about the family, and the circumstances of which I and my brother, my sister and I were born into. I believe differently, and with the new awareness that I now have, I know that I always had that choice—even before I was born.

My birth was not an accident, nor were the circumstances of my arrival into physicality. The birth and parents were perfect for what my higher self wanted to experience in this lifetime. I look back with understanding, not bitterness or regret. It is my desire to move past it all and be healed, and this will allow me to move to an even higher level of understanding.

BOOK TWO

Chapter 5

Faith, Prayers and Malpractice

Now a Pause For Some Anger Management

At this juncture in the book I feel the ice starting to get a bit thin. What I have written so far, and will continue to write about, is my truth. It is what I know. I am not asking anyone to take my truth as their own. It is not my intention to offend anyone, especially anyone who feels they are now enlightened. The truth is it would be impossible to offend one who is enlightened.

Enlightened persons would simply look at what I have written and know that I am not there yet. They would think nothing of it and they would not pass judgment. In fact an enlightened person would simply recognize me as another soul, and would care nothing about what I have written or what I do. If we are truly all one, who would he judge but himself?

This would be a good test for you. If you have found yourself in the place of being offended or angered by what you have read so far, your true feelings are an indicator of where you are spiritually, and maybe this would be a good time to stop reading this book, and take the time to re-evaluate your belief system. Each of us is walking our own path, and no one is better than the other.

Spiritual Malpractice

I will tackle the big ugly words first. Is there such a thing as "*spiritual malpractice,*" and who commits it? How does it apply here?

I explained in the last chapter that it is my belief that we as souls choose to come into the physical realm we call earth, of our own free will. We choose the time of our birth and we choose the parents and the circumstances of our birth. It is not happenstance, and it is purposeful.

The parents we choose give us the best opportunity to manifest the experience in the physical life that the soul desires. The combination of our parent's personalities, and their attributes, are always considered. Once we are born we are on our own to give our lives purpose, and recreate the experience we chose before birth.

We are given the gift of forgetfulness in order to have "free will," as human beings to create ourselves as we see fit.

As a new born, and up to the age of three or four, we are more aware of whom we really are than we ever will be in this life. After this we rapidly start forgetting, as our parents and society moulds us into the image they have for us.

If our free will is in harmony with what the spirit desires, then the body will facilitate the experience it came here for. Because we have forgotten why we came, we spend a lifetime trying to find ourselves, and trying to remember. The soul is always present and always creating circumstances that will give the ego opportunity, that it may realize its purpose. It will never interfere with your choice. When ego becomes aligned with the spirit it will choose the appropriate opportunities for the soul to know itself experientially.

For whatever reason, unknown to us, the soul's purpose may have been to experience a serious illness, and the opportunities that the illness may bring to us. There may be circumstances around the illness that the soul desires to experience. All of life's so called tragedies, or misfortunes, are opportunities for growth. Growth does not come when everything is going well. The challenge, or the struggle, may be the factors which bring out the best in each of us.

When perfection is reached there is no growth. Where there is no growth there is no life, and life is all about change.

So, what if I have a life-threatening illness and I am a loving partner with children? I am well loved in the community, and devote myself to helping others most of my life. I give to charity, and belong to different service organizations. Does this make me immune from illness?

It is all about what is going on in the inside that determines whether you choose sickness or accident. The universe is impartial, and it will manifest whatever it is you choose to be or have. There is no such thing as a deserving or undeserving person in reality, this is a human percept.

When you choose illness as your experience from any level of consciousness, the ego will rationalize it the best it can. What you think of the illness, from the position of being, a sentient being with "free will," will determine the outcome.

Because you have free will, you have many choices as to what your thoughts will be about the circumstances   of   this   ailment.

- This is a great tragedy.
- This is Karma.
- This is a great opportunity for growth.
- This is a natural course of events.
- This is what the soul desired.

Who is to know what the soul wants? Who is there to judge the reasons of the soul, is it on a divine mission? If the person with the life-threatening illness is in harmony with their spirit, they may only have an intuitive thought about it. Unless the root cause for the illness is discovered; there is no chance of lasting remission or cure. You must realize that whatever is going to play out here is purposeful. Even before the time of birth, this is what the soul may have chosen. The body (ego) is not who we are and the soul is the one that is orchestrating. The body facilitates the soul's wishes, but not against the free will of the individual (ego). All three parts of your person, mind, body and spirit—have to be in complete harmony for it to work.

"Prayer for healing should only follow the request of that individual for such healing."—*Herbert Puryear, "The Edgar Cayce Primer."*

What happens when we know of the condition of
this person, and decide to pray for their recovery,
without their permission? When this happens, the
one doing the praying has clearly committed
spiritual malpractice! The prayer, although made
in good faith, may now be interfering with what
the soul is trying to experience. Prayer is powerful
and even more powerful when more than one
person is engaged in the same prayer. With this
kind of interference, the higher purpose of the soul
may not be realized. Another opportunity will be
created by the soul, for its purposes, if
intervention has prematurely interfered with what
it wanted to experience.

With this kind of intervention you have
invalidated the whole purpose for this person
being in this world. The person may get well this
time, but the illness may manifest itself at a later
time.

Before you ever attempt to pray for another
person to be cured, ask yourself honestly who is it
for? Is it for the sake of your own ego or,
genuinely, for the health of the other? If it is truly
for the other, ask their permission.

With good intentions of course, you have made a
serious misjudgment, and have taken the law into
your own hands to heal this person. Now, in case
you missed it, praying "*without*" a person's
permission is the offense, and it is practicing
healing without license to do so, and it is Spiritual
Malpractice.

There is nothing incorrect about praying.
Praying is very beneficial to your health and the

health of others. Praying that the other may manifest what they desire does not require permission of the other, and serves one's own desire to help. Praying for general good health, or protection for another is okay. The other soul can accept that prayer as a gift, and good or poor health is always a choice, it cannot be forced on one. Praying for the recovery of a sick person may not be in the best interest of that person. You must always ask permission of the ill, or injured, person first. If you are unable to ask for permission from the sick person, you must know that the illness is purposeful. Let the situation manifest itself to its conclusion, whether or not you think it *good* or *bad*. If a person asks you to pray for them, and then do so, it is a wonderful opportunity for you to help someone in need.

My daytime job is in outside sales and I am invited into six to eight homes a day. During one of my recent visits with a very nice couple, we briefly touched on the subject of spiritualism. In any business this is a taboo. There are three things you never talk about with a customer—sex, politics or religion.

I blew it big time with this couple, and they tried to rip me to shreds with an amazing display of their Biblical oratory. If I was interested in finding out more about the Bible perhaps they would be the ones I would turn to. They are both strong Catholics and have been devoted to living in that box for a very long time; they were not open to any different ideas. I did not argue with them about their convictions, but I did give them a brief introduction into my beliefs, which added more fuel to the fire.

I politely sat, and listened, until I finally had to cut it short with, "I must move onto my next appointment." I left in good terms with them, but on the way out the wife said that she would pray for me. Since she didn't ask for my permission, I asked her not to. With true Christian arrogance, and a display of disrespect, she said she would anyway, in spite of my objection.

I believe this is one of the most egotistical statements a person could make. To assume to know what another soul's purpose is, is more than arrogant, it is extremely presumptuous, and negates the souls purpose. It is a pompous attitude that comes from someone living in a box, and certainly is atypical of any enlightened person.

Jesus himself would recognize the sovereignty of another soul and respect it. I do not remember anywhere in the Bible where Jesus forced his will on anyone. Those who desired healing or help, sought him out, and they came to him. All were welcome to listen, and his appearances were never advertised. No one was solicited by him to hear his words, they came of their own free will. Only mankind would impose his words and beliefs on others. Spiritual *malpractice* does not work in any kind of healing.

Prayer

"The correct prayer is therefore never a prayer of supplication, but a prayer of gratitude."—RA Clark, "The Christ Mind."

To pray for a thing is to give thanks for already having it. Gratitude is the "Great Secret," to having prayers answered. When you pray for money, you are saying to the universe that you don't have any, and that's exactly what you get back nothing. When you give thanks for your abundance, which is the message you send out, that is what you get back abundance. The universe is resonant of your words, and responds in kind.

The spoken word is the most powerful aspect of the three steps to successful creation. Thought, word and deed, in that order. All physical objects are symbols of a thought process. Thank the creator for your good health, that is what you will get back. If you pray for health, you are saying you don't have good health. That is what you will get back. Be careful what you pray for, you will get it.

Never pray for something that you want, give thanks for already having it. Wanting is what you will always get back, if your prayer is one of lack.

"In creation of individual reality, thought control or what some might call prayer—is everything."— *Neale Donald Walsch, "Conversations with God, Book Three."*

Chapter 6

Healing Methodology

"We're all of us ill in one way or another: We call it health when we find no symptom."—
T.S. Eliot

Another Pause

I am not asking you for a leap of faith in this chapter. It is just not necessary. I am not asking anything of you, except that you keep an open mind, and try to learn something new which may be of benefit to you.

If what you now know has brought you good mental and physical health, or some healing in your life, as well as for those around you, and the world, there would be little need of you reading any further. There would be no point to it, unless you wanted to learn something new that may add meaning to your life. This book was not written to insult your intelligence, but to enhance what you already know.

You were, intentionally, brought to this point in the book for a reason, and it may only have been to reaffirm that what you already know as your truth works for you. In that case the book was purposeful. It may also be that there is a question that you have that can only be answered by reading farther. Recognize the opportunity as a gift and accept it with gratitude. For you are getting what you asked for at some level.

Holism or Holistic Healing

"The treatment of any subject as a whole integrated system, esp., in medicine, the consideration of the complete person, physically and psychologically, in the treatment of disease."—
The Collins English Dictionary

Holistic healing may be as outlined, an awakening the desire to be one with the whole. There is no condition that cannot be healed by aligning your will with that pattern. To summarize, a major element of health of our physical bodies is an attitude of caring.

Both New Age and New Thought movements endorse the treatment of the whole person, when treating any given symptoms, and the use of orthodox medicine when appropriate, with New Thought relying more exclusively on spiritual healing.

"Holistic healing may now be defined as awakening the desire to be one with the Whole."— *Herbert B. Puryear, "The Edgar Cayce Primer."*

Yoga is an example of holistic healing. It is a Hindu system that uses ongoing physical and mental exercise programs for wellness, and it treats the whole body.

The idea of holism is that if you stub your toe, the whole body is going to know about it, and is going to need treatment at some level.

Holistic healing incorporates many sub forms of specialized healing for the whole body including, reflexology, reiki, aromathy, chiropractic, osteopathy, shiatsu, Zen meditation, Rolfing, and more.

Orthodox medicines, for the most part, treat localized symptoms and are, most often, toxic with minor or serious side affects that do damage to the rest of the body. It's analogous to hitting your thumb with a hammer so you don't feel the tooth ache.

You came from the perfect body, that which is whole. The separation from the whole has led you to believe that you are less than the whole, less perfect. Your individuality or "free will" has allowed you to believe this. Only the truth about who you really are will set you free, will bring you back to wholeness.

Faith Healers

In dealing with faith healings it is required of the one to be healed to completely submit to the healer. The healing is externalized and the patient must believe that the healing is coming from, or through, the one performing the healing ritual.

The one receiving the healing is often pumped up into an altered state of hysteria, either induced through ritual or drugs. They must have faith in the healer to perform, and believe in him, and only him, as a channel through which a greater power works.

Although the sick one may show signs of being cured in the moment, or even experience a complete recovery, most times this is temporary. It can not be a lasting cure, because the thought for the illness was never changed—the cure was not holistic. The condition may re-appear in another re-incarnation, unless the root thought has changed.

As a six year old child with Perthes disease, I watched the Oral Roberts crusades on television. Sunday mornings would find me on the couch with cast on, and glued to the TV screen. I marveled at the people that would come to the big tent and then, at the end of the program, go to the front for instant healing. Some walked on crutches or cane, while others maneuvered through the crowd in wheel chairs—all believing they would be cured of their ailments.

It all seemed so simple; you just had to be there. Oral Roberts would put his hands on the people, yell out a few worlds, and the crippled would rise up and dance. Others would throw their crutches to the floor and walk away.

As an innocent young boy watching this on television, I knew that I wanted to go see Oral Roberts and get healed. I doubted that the trip would ever happen, but I was totally inspired by what I saw, and I realized that it was possible for me to walk again. Sometimes my mother would sit beside me, and we would watch together. I understood from the family that she had told them she sometimes could feel my body vibrating while I watched the show. I believe that she must have had some faith, or intuition, that a miracle was going to happen.

Osteopathy and Chiropractic

> "Osteopathy is a system of healing based on the manipulation of bones or other parts of the body."—
> The Collins English Dictionary

Osteopathy is based on not only adjusting the spine, but also improving circulation. Osteopathy is a technique for coordinating the nervous systems of the body. The blood carries nutrients and oxygen to the cells of the body and carries away waste and toxins. Manipulation of the bones, by way of osteopathy, increases circulation and removes blockages. Massage enhances circulation in the lymphatic system, which aids in purifying the blood and increase immunity.

Supporting Prayer

I touched on prayer earlier in the book, and there has been much written about prayer. The only true prayer is said to be "Thy Will be done," and "Thy Will," is your will. If you can not think of anything else, this short prayer will cover everything.

Prayer is universal. It crosses all boundaries, and we pray instinctually. It is non-denominational, and flows naturally from our thoughts. Whether we know it or not we pray every day. Even a one word prayer like "damn," is a short prayer. It says I made a mistake, help me fix it or help me not do it again. Help me make it right. At some level of consciousness our soul knows what they are part of, and it longs to communicate with source. Although we may not know what to call it, we all know there is another part of ourselves we should be communing with.

Prayer is an affirmation of circumstances and experiences going on in our lives now. We are really communing with ourselves to a subconscious level, and reporting on things that have manifested in our physical lives. Unfortunately, most prayers we make are prayers of lack, and that is why we *don't* get what we are praying for. The infinite does not arbitrarily grant some prayers and not others. The creator is impersonal and cannot make the distinction between deserving and undeserving. It, therefore has no choice but to give us what we pray for.

Prayers of affirmation will lead us into attunement with the spirit within, and direct the energy forces where healing is needed. If I pray to have my condition healed it will not happen, because I am making a statement or prayer of lack. I am saying that I have this physical condition and the universe is resonant of my word. I will get back to the reality of still having the ailment.

If I say a prayer of gratitude for already having been healed or having perfect health, that will also resonate through the universe, and come back to me as my new reality. As I get closer to the infinite which is "whole," I become whole. It can not happen any other way, because I am part of the whole as I merge back with it, I become as it is, everything that it is.

Meditation

Meditation is the channel, the doorway to the soul. Meditation facilitates attunement with the Infinite. *Meditation* and *Prayer* work together. There is an expression, "We pray to meditate and we meditate in order to pray." *Prayers of preparation* lead us to greater accordance. As the spirit is raised it may interact with those of another. Meditation is as close as we can get with the infinite in this life form.

Often meditation is ineffective because we are not fully prepared with prayers that have primed us. Because meditation is part of a holistic approach to healing it touches everyone, the meditator and the one to be healed—everyone. The thoughts or energy of the one meditating, or praying, facilitates the healing process in the one being healed. The true energy for healing is within the one to be healed, and the prayer may only act as a beacon, or trigger that will activate the healing process within the individual. It may provide the pattern of life or wholeness to be followed.

There are many different ways to meditate—and no one way is the *right* one. I have been meditating for almost thirty years. The first method I learned was Transcendental Meditation, and I have practiced it the most. I have learned other ways since. I practice with tapes and without, in silence and in crowds. I have spent a lot of money on the Centrepointe Awakening System to learn how to meditate deeper than a Zen monk. I cannot say with any conviction, that I have made any great inroads with any of these systems. This does not mean that meditation does not work for me. It simply means that the methods of meditation are not working.

The most effective way I have found to meditate is what I call a "waking meditation through creativity." I got lost in myself as a musician when I played the drums in a band. I get lost within myself as I write this book, and other things that I have written. I have worked as an electronics technician as well as a refrigeration and appliance tech. During the process of repairing anything, I get lost within myself and become unaware of time. That does not happen for me during what I call sleeping meditation, sitting in a lotus position repeating a mantra.

Meditation can happen anywhere, we all do it. We may stop and admire the beauty of a flower garden, or something in nature, and suddenly realize that we were off somewhere in space. It is a natural thing to do. Timelessness is often an indication that we have been meditating. That can happen in a conversation or even working on the computer. Have you ever tried to get on for 15 minutes and two or three hours later you realize you've lost track of time.

During meditation you are becoming attuned to the Infinite, and are present in the eternal moment of now. Your brain cannot operate in the present moment. It operates only in the past and the future. During meditation you experience wholeness; you cannot dwell on anything physical because it does not exist in that state of awareness. Meditation should be experienced daily. Time put aside to commune with your soul brings immeasurable benefits.

I have meditated for up to three hours a day in a sleeping meditation practiced at different times during the day. This is a personal preference—

only two, 15-minute periods a day is all that is needed to start to experience the results of getting closer to that which created you.

The benefits of meditation are many, but the true nature of meditation is an opportunity to commune with your creator. To do otherwise is like saying to the one you love, I promise to love you if you give me this or that, and it is conditional on getting what you want. Unconditional love works both ways. In order for it to work you must expect unconditional love and give unconditional love. If you are only focused on the results then eventually you will be disappointed because you will have missed out on the opportunity to communicate with the *infinite*. That is the reason or purpose for meditating—to commune with the creator, the one that created you. Do not go into meditation expecting something in return. Expect to be with your creator, and the benefits will come to you as part of the process, as it does in all loving relationships.

If you never talk to the one in your life whom you love, you do not have a real relationship with that person. Meditation is a portal, a doorway from this physical existence to that which has created you, and the other two-thirds of who you really are. It is the phone line to heaven, your high speed connection. Can you image how well a captain would be able to run his ship if he could not talk to the rest of his crew? The ship would be in chaos in a short period of time.

Communication is life-assuring in any community, and brings with it intimacy and bonding, whether it is your immediate family, your neighbourhood, or the triune which is you. If there were no communication between the cells of your body you would cease to exist. There is constant communication between the electrons of atoms, and other subatomic particles, that makes up the body you believe yourself to be. Communication is essential for healing. It carries the pattern for life for wholeness, to all parts of your body. Healing comes with "right" communication. Think healthy and pass it on to the rest of your body. This life-affirming communication in your body is also shared between souls. It is transmitted from your physical body to all those around you, and throughout the universe. Any thought you have ever had still exists somewhere in the universe. This information is shared by all souls.

Sleep

Healthy sleep may be one of the most neglected elements of a wholesome body and mind. In Jane Roberts' book, "Seth Speaks," Seth recommends having five hours of sleep, ideally, at a time with which you gain the maximum benefit. Those who require more sleep may take a two-hour nap, or some other combination. It is not beneficial to have the body inactive for eight to ten hours in a row. Adjusting sleeping patterns will bring many benefits in your life.

A Short Introduction into Quantum Mechanics

I am going to touch on some theories in Physics and Quantum Mechanics. I am going to try and demonstrate, very simplistically, how we can use a system of non-healing to heal what we observe to be sick.

I am not a physicist and I don't pretend to know that much about it, but I find it fascinating. Both the New Thought and The New Age movements embrace quantum mechanics to explain some of the unexplainable. It is not necessary to understand these theories but it will help in understanding, what I call, the non-healing, healing.

Basically, what has been determined through quantum mechanics is that all probabilities exist simultaneously. When one of these probabilities is observed, all the other probabilities collapse, as in the "Schrödinger Wave Equation." In our three dimensional world only one probability can be observed or measured at a time, even though other measuring devices may have recorded other events simultaneously and the first measurement to be observed is the observation that is our reality.

In layman's terms, when we leave the house in the morning to go to work. We have two probabilities when we get to the end of the driveway, unless we have predetermined our direction. Once we make up our mind to turn right, the option to turn left collapses at the instant we made the decision. The second part to this scenario is that theoretically because all probabilities exist at the same time, there was another of us that turned left as well. Both events happened at precisely the same time, both probabilities existed, and both events actualized.

Let's try it another way, very simplistically of course. Should I walk into a candy store, even before I get there, there will be an infinite number of choices to make. Not ever having candy before and having no preferences there will be an equal probability that I would choose any of them.

At the instance that I chose the red jelly bean, the probability that I would choose any of the others collapses and this is observable. I can, of course repeat the experiment and make a different choice, as many times as I desire. It is not the candy that is disappearing only the probability of choosing another once a choice is made.

Because time and space is an illusion in our reality, all probabilities of choice have all have been made simultaneously. There are other probabilities of Roy choosing the other candies at the same time. All candies have therefore been selected. It is within my reality, only that I experience picking the red one.

Because I live in the physical world where time and space exist as an illusion, I can personally experience a repetition of the experiment, one

candy at a time. I have an infinite number of
choices but can experience only a single choice,
within the single probability of my existence.

"Non-healing," Healing

The preceding quantum theory lends itself well
with that of "Religious Science"—theories about
healing.

All conditions of wellness exist at the same time
for any of us. There is a Roy who is perfectly
healthy, and there are other instances of myself
that exist at the same time, with different
probabilities of health. For instance, there is a Roy
who is in the last stages of terminal cancer and
there is another who is in remission, as there is
another that is in the beginning stages and all
other stages in between.

Through an error in thinking I have, at some
level, chose to be in one of those stages of illness,
as opposed to staying healthy. Through the
process of manifesting thought into my reality I
will choose another probability with equal chances
of going one direction or the other.

As I declare from knowingness that I have
cancer, all the other probabilities collapse, until I
again declare something else. Until my thinking
changes, I will keep going in a certain direction of
being healthy or less healthy, or maybe back and
forth from being in the last stages of my illness or
in complete remission. It also follows that if I

declare from knowingness that I do not have cancer, then the probability that I do collapses.

In his book "The Science of Mind," Ernest Holmes explains the New Thought method of healing which I have called non-healing.

As "Science of Mind" healers, practitioners are coached not to think about the patient's illness. To do so only gives it life. One is recognizing the illness and that helps manifest it into the patient's reality. It not only becomes manifest, or is real to the patient, but to the healer as well.

The effective method of healing used in "Science of Mind," is to heal the healer. The practitioner begins by shifting the focus from the patient to himself. He does not recognize the person as being ill. He only knows the patient as being whole or well. As a practitioner, the shift in focus is to the *other probable person* that is well. This theory suggests that the sick Roy, for example, will always exist as a probability, as will all the other probabilities of health and illness. As a healer I am not really healing anyone but bringing the probability of the healthy Roy into my reality.

> *All probabilities of health for Roy exist. At some level, Roy will experience every level of illness. As a practitioner, it is my job to adjust my reality to only know the Roy that is at the wellness end of the scale.*

As I move away from the wellness end of the scale, I move towards illness and eventually death.

This kind of healing can be very impersonal. As a practitioner I don't even have to know you or have ever seen you. All I need to know is your name which is Roy, and the only Roy I know is completely healthy.

The more I am focused on it, the greater the chances that I will make it manifest in my reality. The more this is supported by everyone in the patient's actuality, the more likely the results. The patient must be in complete accord with this healing, and it can not go against his wishes at any level.

As in my earlier example of the toothache, once forgotten there was no pain, until someone reminded him that he had a toothache.

> "No matter what may be the subjective state of our thoughts, the conscious state can change it."—
>
> *Ernest Holmes, "The Science of Mind."*

When I was younger I managed this healing thing with greater ease. I moved from my illness in every probability, back to the point where I was walking again.

Now as I get older, this kind of non-healing has become a little more difficult. In the innocence of my youth I was not burdened with the weight of the baggage that I now carry. The world told me over and over again, in as many ways, that I can not do it. I have partially believed it, and have forgotten how natural it is to be well. From time to time I have moved away from wellness, but not so far that I couldn't get back

As I get older it is becoming even easier to rationalize degradation from age and poor choices in my younger days. I am often reminded by family, and people who know me, that I am not as young as I used to be.

I met a very nice older lady several years ago and we had a bit of a conversation about getting old, and about not doing some of the things we liked to do in our younger days. This lady was young at heart and told me the "*Great Secret of Aging.*" "If you don't want to get old, then don't act your age."

It is in your head. Ask an older person if their soul feels old. They will tell you that it feels the same now as it did years ago. The soul doesn't age—only the body does. It has been observed that people who read a lot, and have moved farther along the spiritual path of enlightenment, actually start looking younger. They have raised their body vibration to a higher level, and the burden of gravity does not weigh them down as much as the body reacts positively to it.

For me to cure my own negative image I must know myself as a positive, healthy person. I can not do this by practicing denial. For healing to occur I must recognize who I am now. I can not give away that which I do not own. I must know where I am first, before I can go anywhere else, so I must surrender first. Surrendering is the key

factor to moving on, and if you are still carrying
the old baggage, you are not going very far.

To be conscious of illness is to know it, is to give
it life, it is an error in thinking. Once you have it,
you cannot rid yourself of it by denying its
existence. Know that you had it, and let it go.
Sickness is an illusion that you have brought into
your life for a purpose. Find the purpose and
change your thoughts about it.

When we think of ourselves in poor light we see
only the darkness. We must clean house of poor
thoughts, before we can heal ourselves and those
around us, and the world community.

What I have brought to you in this book is not
trickery, or slight of hand, it has all been created
by you. The three steps to manifesting are
thoughts word and deed. Think only healthy, say
only healthy things, and be healthy. Know that
what I have just told you is a universal,
impersonal law of nature and it must be obeyed.
No one is unworthy; this natural law will operate
for anyone. When you become attuned to the
infinite, you become as the infinite. You can use
the universal laws to get what you desire in
greater degrees.

The fastest way to get what you desire is to
know that you already have it. In your prayers,
always give thanks for already having what you
desire.

The slowest way to get what you want is to think
that it comes from somewhere, or somebody else.
The more you externalize, the less likely you will
get what you want.

BOOK TWO

Chapter 7

The "Great Secret," Revealed

The "Great Secret" was really never really a secret after all. You have known it all along you simply forgot, and that is the truth—we all forgot. We all forgot who we are, and what power we have over our own lives. In fact, we are the only ones with any power over our lives. If you haven't picked up on it yet, then know this, YOU DON'T HAVE TO BE SICK... YOU CREATE AND MANIFEST YOUR OWN ILLNESS OR ACCIDENTS.

If you don't want to be sick, then be healthy. Sickness is a state of being, you are being sick. It is an erroneous way of thinking that has manifested itself into something unnatural. Sickness is not your natural state; you have to work at being sick. Make whatever changes are necessary to eliminate the cause of your destructive thinking. Disease in not a spiritual reality, it is an experience, but not a truth.

If you hate illness you may bring upon yourself a succeeding life of illness, because the hate has drawn it to you. If you expand your awareness of health, love and being, then you are drawn to these qualities. A generation that hates war will not bring peace. A generation that loves peace will bring peace.

We are all healers, each and every one of us. We all have, within us, the power to heal. Heal ourselves, others and the world. By knowing our "truth," the truth about whom we really are, we carry that knowledge with us and we share it with others. We have come to the room to heal the room. We have come to the space to heal the space.

There really is only one lesson in this book, and there is only one basic thought that is woven into each paragraph. That is "Healthy mind, Healthy Body." Although you may have symptoms that show up in only one part of your body, the whole body suffers and needs to be treated. Illness is all inclusive—the "whole" suffers through any of its parts. If you have ever experienced a headache, or toothache, you will remember that your whole body suffered.

Your body is not who you are, it is just a vehicle for your soul to experience itself in the three-dimensional world. If your body shows signs of illness, it is an outward manifestation of an inward thought process may be unhealthy. You can never be fully healed until you find the cause of the illness which may be psychological. Your body is merely telling you something about that is going on inside. Listen to it! Being ill is an illusion, and it can have some very real physical consequences. Note the signs and treat the mind.

Non-critical illnesses that are observable most often represent problems that are being worked out, and are brought into the open.

Symptoms can be part of the healing process in these cases. Outward symptoms give us the opportunity to search inward, to find out what is represented by the symptoms, and to measure our progress by them. Symptoms that remain partially or wholly hidden may represent inner problems that we may not be ready to deal with or face, so the symptoms remain hidden. At a much higher level of understanding, symptoms may be carryovers from another life that wasn't dealt with. Sometimes patients will report these symptoms, and doctors cannot find anything physically wrong.

Your health is a physical observation, or feedback system, of the wellness of your inner personality.

In Conclusion

To become a channel of healing, it is important to know that you are not here to fix or rescue people. This is very close to being judgmental. Effective healing only comes from knowing a person as, "well." You cannot judge them, nor try to help them without permission, because you don't know their soul's purpose.

For healing to occur there must be a oneness in purpose between the person praying, and the one for whom the prayer is being offered. To pray for one with lung cancer, without the person being willing to quit smoking, would be of little purpose.

Wholeness is a process of becoming attuned mentally and physically with the spirit. It is our nature in spirit to be one with the creator, the universe, our neighbours, and one with ourselves. It is natural to move to a higher level of awareness to wholeness. We were never meant to get sick, or have accidents. There is a pattern of wholeness within each and every one of us, to function in a normal and healthy manner.

When you are standing in the middle of a swamp and you are surrounded by alligators, it is very hard to take the time to think about why you are there. There is something you must do about it now.

When a small boy falls and skins his knee, he wants it kissed better, and then move on to what he was doing before. He wants immediate relief from his pain.

In our fast-moving society we are all looking for quick fixes to everything, including ill health. We want the cure now and it seems that while we are working to find a cure for one disease, another has cropped up. Why is that?

The reason is observable, we have lost our way. We have forgotten that we are part of a world community. When one part hurts the whole world suffers for it. We cannot isolate our illnesses. They keep popping up all around us. We must treat the whole body, change the way the world views itself, before any of us can expect to live in perfect health. We can no longer indulge ourselves in the illusion of separation.

We are one, one with each other, and one with the world we live in. What ever happens in Iraq, the Middle East, China, or anywhere else will affect us here. Wherever there is poverty or inequity, prejudice or indifference among men, women or nations, there will be sickness.

In the consciousness of God, there is no sickness, imperfection or death. The more you walk on the path of God consciousness, the sooner you will be perfect again.

The thought process of the group is faulty, and again the whole body will suffer.

Through negative thinking, we create our so called "natural" disasters. We create our droughts, our forest fires and floods, hurricanes and infestations. As the world body thinks disaster, doom and gloom, tragedy, war and separation, that is what we will attract and manifest.

There are no innocent victims, bystanders or perpetrators. We are all guilty, and we create it *en masse* because that is what we think about, that is what is in our minds. Don't try to treat the symptoms, treat the whole body, and start with the mind.

You can't save it, or hoard it or hide it. Eventually you will have to share it, or lose it all together. There is no place to hide—who would you be hiding from. Can you believe that you could hide from yourself? There are over 6.5 billion manifestations of yourself worldwide and they are all intimately connected at some level.

Start the healing now, start with the very next thought in your head, and bring forth the cure by knowing there is no one else to do it. There can be no finger pointing, no passing the buck. You are the creator manifesting "individually" in this, your physical body. We are creating a world illness, "collectively" and spreading it around the globe. Mother earth is becoming sick, who will kiss it better? Stop it now!

We don't get stung by a mosquito that has malaria by accident. We don't get run over by a car by accident, and we are not killed by a terrorists by accident. There are no such things as accidents—only probabilities that we have created, and are waiting to experience. At some level of our consciousness we will choose one of those possibilities, and create the circumstance that will put us into the right place, at the right time, in order to experience it. Nothing is by chance, or accident. It was all created by design, by you. If you don't like your life's experience, change it. You are in control. You are not a victim of circumstance, you are creating it.

BOOK THREE

SIMPLE MANIFESTING

Introduction

In the last five years, I have become fascinated with the natural process of manifesting. Manifesting is something that we all do very well, and most of the time at a subconscious level. When we reflect back on different parts of our lives, or those of others, we can see how perfectly everything has fallen into place. All of the steps that were necessary to get you to an imagined place in your life, have been mapped out in an exquisite orchestration that rivals any symphony.

I say imagined because it is a "thought" that first triggers the imagination, that triggers a desire to have, do or be a thing. It is then the spoken word that declares it to be the thing that you want to be, do or have, then if it is focused upon long enough, it comes into manifestation, into your experience.

The world is a stage you are both the director and the player. This physical world is a wonderful adventure playground that was created for you to experience yourselves (who you really are) in physical form. You are entirely unlimited in what you can create. You were given *"carte blanche,"* and free will to recreate anything and everything and you do that individually and *en masse*.

There are no prizes, Oscars or any other rewards. Neither are there any punishments—at the spiritual level—for what you create. You are an unlimited spirit, experiencing the joy of creating and living its own magnificence. The process of manifesting is unbelievably simple, but not easy, given whom we think we are. Because manifesting is so simple, it is very difficult for most of us to do it on a conscious level—we believe that it is too simple to work. Our ego or personality gets in the way of manifesting the things we most desire, because we try too hard, and do not let the system work for us. I will try to reveal the contradiction in the forthcoming chapters. I have started the book with several stories, including my own. In these stories I hope that you will see, in hindsight, how situations are created for us in perfect order, so that the spirit may realize its purpose.

The first story demonstrates that when we are single-minded and focused, we will always get what we want. The age makes no difference. Some of us are lucky enough to know what we want, from the time we are born, and we start thinking independently. The things that happen, seemingly by chance, are purposeful, and will lead to the next step in manifesting the experiences that we desire. I have heard many other stories of young people that have grown up to become what they imagined. They all have had such determination—no one could ever doubt they would succeed.

The second story is a true story about a close friend of mine. The name in the story has been changed at his request. This man's story is typical of a person with a positive outlook, who knows that he will always get what he wants. Harvey is a middle class worker, he lives in a middle class house, in a middle class neighbourhood. His wife and he both work. There is very little that Harvey longs for. Harvey is comfortable; he does not have lots of money, but with his investments he will retire comfortably. He has manifested the life he desired, and it is the classical, home, wife, kids and dogs. These were the things that he was taught to attach value to.

Vicky's story is unique. I have never seen anyone manifest as well as she can. She can almost do it on demand, like "poof," it is there. Conscious manifesting requires a high level of belief in the system. It is only recently that Vicky has learned to understand the mechanics of the system.

Like most of us she just took life for granted. Vicky came from a middle class family in Hong Kong. In her early thirties, she has not settled down, and continues to reach out for new experiences. She expects to be successful, to have lots of money, and she expects to be happy. So far, this is what she has manifested, and she has left very clear tracks.

Part of my own story is in Chapter Four. I have never been comfortable with talking about it. When I look back over the last 55 years of my life, my ego would say it was a struggle. I believe I have had to work much harder than those in the other stories. There is nothing wrong with that, it is what was chosen at some level, and it was purposeful. Consciously, I would not have chosen the path I took.

When I read autobiographies of some of the great spiritual writers, I noticed that many of them had difficult lives. The other thing most of them have in common is the gratitude they expressed for their lives, lived. I strongly recommend the books, "A Boy Called It" and "A Man Named Dave," by author Dave Pelzer. This man was subject to the worst case of child abuse anyone could imagine, and yet he says he is grateful for what happened to him.

It is not difficult to look back on a life cycle and see the pattern that was there. By doing so, you can appreciate that the pattern in your life is one that you were creating yourself. The choices we make daily manifest the outcome. The choices or opportunities are put there by another part of ourselves on a subconscious level. It is the ego that makes the final decision. Look into the lives of the ones I have written about, then look at the patterns in your life, and know that they can be changed at anytime. If you do not like what you are experiencing, the patterns can be changed at any   time,   by   choice.

Chapter 1

The Story of Jerry

Today, Jerry is a senior pilot for a major airline, and flies jumbo jets all over the world. When he is not flying jets, he spends most of his time flying his little Cessna around the Fraser Valley with his small dog Roger, often his daughter Sarah, or friends.

Jerry loves his job, and from the time he could remember, flying is all he ever wanted to do. The choices and circumstance that lead him to the realization of his dreams seemed difficult at the time. In hindsight, Jerry reflects on how obvious the whole journey was, and how simply and beautifully the process works, despite what he may have thought at the time.

Jerry was born in a small town in British Columbia, Canada, called Chilliwack. The family was very poor. Jerry's dad worked on local farms to earn barely enough money to sustain the family. Jerry's parents never owned their own home. They frequently moved in and around their small community, usually in concert with the property owners raising the rent. From time to time, they lived out of boxes, never staying in one place very long. They acquired few peaces of furniture—some of it Jerry father built from scrap pieces of wood. Given the circumstances, Jerry's parents were content with the way they lived.

There were few disagreements and a lot of hard work. The parents were both the same age and they had Jerry was born during the year of their 23rd birthdays.

While still a baby in a crib built by his father a small mobile was hung over the crib to keep him amused. The mobile consisted of a small model airplane that Jerry's Dad carved from wood, with bi-wings and a moving propeller. This labour of love was suspended on a string, and affixed to the side of his crib. During the long summer days, his mother would keep the window open in the bedroom for fresh air, and the wind would drive the propeller and the mobile around in circles over Jerry's head. Jerry would laugh, and make gurgling sounds at the free flying aircraft.

When the sounds of laughter turned to crying, Jerry's mother knew that the wind had subsided, and the mobile had come to rest. She often used it to lull him to sleep at night, and propel him off into a far away journey above the clouds, free of the gravity that pressed him to the mattress of his crib.

As Jerry grew, his fascination with airplanes blossomed into a craving to collect, and build, models of his own. Christmas and birthday presents often brought delivery of yet another plane to add to his expanding fleet of aircraft. Jerry favoured smaller conventional planes, as to military aircraft. The refrigerator door was always home to another of his best airplane drawings, etched out on paper with crayon.

As Jerry discovered that people flew those planes, and that every planes, and every plane had a pilot in it, he insisted that he would be a pilot some day. There was no talking him into being a firefighter, or police officer, as the other boys dreamed of. Jerry knew he would be a pilot some day.

His father bemoaned the likelihood of any opportunity ever coming up to pay for his son's flight school. He could barely pay the rent, and put food on the table. There were not a lot of opportunities in the Valley for someone to make a career out of flying, and lessons were too expensive. As with most of the other boys, he would most likely work on a farm. This did not sway Jerry, he was determined to be a pilot, even at that young age, and he knew he would find a way to get his wings. He simply would not be talked into considering anything else.

Jerry had never seen an airplane close up, except for the occasional crop duster that would fly low over the house.

He dreamed someday about walking up to one, touching it and, God permit, the greatest joy of all—he would be allowed to climb into the cockpit. He imagined how it would feel. He could hear the sounds of the engine starting up, and feel the vibrations running through his body as the engine revved up in anticipation of takeoff. Instructions from the control tower came over the radio as he taxied to the runway, and finally, "you are now cleared for takeoff." Jerry knew that phrase very well. His mother used that line for years when she tucked him into bed at night. She would say, "OK Jerry, you are now cleared for takeoff have a great flight." Off to sleep Jerry would go.

Jerry would run through the checklist with his dad, when they hopped into the pickup to go to town. Gas check, air pressure check, mirrors check, keys in ignition check, and ready for takeoff, check.

Just before Jerry's seventh birthday, the landlord stopped in with the all too familiar news that the rent on the house had to be increased to cover expenses. This was always followed by another move, when a house of lower rent could be found. The family had moved so many times that rental places were starting to be scarce, and it would not be easy to find one they could afford.

During a trip into town the family truck broke down, and had to be towed into the garage. The timing of still another expense was not welcomed. As the pickup was lowered from the tow truck, his father shuffled around the office waiting for the bad news about the necessary repairs. He noticed the bulletin board on the wall, and made his way over to glance at the local notices and ads. On a small piece of brown paper pinned to the board was an ad for a rental house. It read, "Low rent, two bedroom house on old road to airport, noisy at times but reasonable rent, immediate occupancy, call..."

The family moved in the following week, with one pick-up truck load of furniture and household belongings. Jerry was not told where they were moving, and he never asked. He was used to the moving, and one place was the same as the other. As they drove toward the municipal airport, the light planes rose just barely above the top of the truck, when they lifted off, from the runway. The old truck ambled down the tapered country road that paralleled the east/west runway. Jerry, with his head hanging out the window, watched every take off and landing, and he commented on the pilots' abilities as they approached the runway.

Jerry's feet did not touch the ground as he flew from the truck when it finally came to a halt in front of their new home. Nor did he take notice of the house. He ran to the fence that aligned the runway, ignoring the calls of both his parents. He had just landed in heaven, and found himself standing at the gates. His parents left him at the fence for the remainder of the day, while they settled into the house. It was not until supper was called that he finally tore himself away.

Jerry spent most of that summer sitting crossed legged at the edge of the fence, or high on a branch in the old maple tree that rested near the corner of the house, watching the planes land and take off. In the evenings, while lying on his back in his bed with his hands folded under his head, he listened to the sounds of the planes' engines. He learned the sounds of the different planes, and could identify them as local planes or not. Every so often, a pilot would cut his engine too soon, and Jerry would spring from his bed to the window to make sure it made a successful landing.

After several months in their new location, the family got used to the noise of the airport. Most of the time they did not hear the planes landing and taking off. Jerry never missed one take off or landing, and always had a comment about the make of the plane as it raced by the house. He was never allowed to venture onto airport property, and would often come into the house with the impression of the chain link on his face or forehead.

Jerry knew that he would make it to the hangers one day when he got a little older, perhaps next year. There was no other place he would rather be. He would get close to one and touch it and he would remember the joy of that first experience for the rest of his life.

In readiness of that day, Jerry studied airplanes with a passion. He spent time at the school library, and would read anything about airplanes. He studied their schematics and specifications. All his drawings in school were of airplanes. He would even design new models; they were often posted on the refrigerator door at home. Some were all too obvious on the classroom windows, and on the inside of his workbooks.

Jerry was often reprimanded for flying paper airplanes within the confines of the school building. His classmates would get him into trouble, regularly, by creating the paper planes and flying them in the classrooms and hallways and then blaming it on him. Notes that were sent home to his parents usually came in the shape of an airplane folded from the paper. They would glide to a gentle stop at the end of the runway on the kitchen table. The scolding from parents and teachers never influenced his behaviour. Writing lines, and cleaning the schoolyard, gave him time to daydream even more. The kids grew bored with teasing him and seldom included him in their play. They finally got the message and left him alone.

By the end of Jerry's second year of school, he had already built a reputation as a future pilot. There were those that admired his expertise on flying and aircraft, and an equal amount of those either indifferent or tired of hearing about it. He was both accepted by some and admonished by others, Much of his time was spent running around the schoolyard with arms outstretched, coming in for a landing or taking off.

Jerry was good with his hands and his dad had taught him how to use tools. At the age of eight, Jerry had already built his first child-sized airplane, and was eager to experience his very first test flight. Built out of cardboard and wood, it was light, and should easily glide to a soft landing from the roof of their home. Weeks had gone by in its design and fabrication. This week would be the inaugural flight of 'Spirit One.'

Early Sunday morning Jerry left the house to prepare for the test flight. He walked to an old shed that he had used for a hanger. He strapped on his pilots hat, wrapped a scarf around his neck, and secured a backpack to himself with a make-shift parachute inside. A big part of being a pilot is looking like a pilot. Jerry opened the hanger door, and wheeled "Spirit One," out into the first rays of the early morning sun.

From a high branch, off the maple tree that leaned against the corner of the house, Jerry raised "Spirit One," to the roof, and positioned it strategically facing into the wind, in the direction of the airfield. He anticipated a smooth take off, and a short flight to the soft grass below. Jerry had already calculated the direction of the wind. and the approximate speed—conditions were perfect for take off. His heart now racing as he climbed into the cockpit, it would be now or never.

He waited for the next gust of wind, and then shifted his weight, so that the aircraft would move down the old wood shakes of the roof.

The best part of the ride was from the peak of the roof to the gutter. From there on it was straight down. Jerry let out a scream of pain as 'Spirit One' folded into a lump of broken wood and bent cardboard, against the chain link fence. His mother, hearing his screams, rushed out to find him sitting in the middle of the wreckage unable to raise his arm. Jerry was rushed to the hospital with a broken collarbone. His only comment was, "I did it, I flew."

Jerry was grounded from flying planes off the roof. He promised there would be no more such experiments with airplanes. However, he was very careful not to include parachutes in his promise.

This would not be the only time that Jerry would try his hand at flying. He would also try his hand at making a parachute. His mother's umbrella was the next casualty. One of his bed sheets with corners tied by twine to his belt, did not slow his decent to the ground. A large plastic bag used to ship the refrigerator may have worked if the closed end had not blown out on its first try. Two or three tries did not yield good results, and that design was retired.

Jerry reasoned that a ten-foot drop was not enough for some of these parachutes to open. A longer drop was necessary. A new location from perhaps a barn with a steep roof, would produce the desired results. It would have to wait for now, as there were no buildings nearby. He resigned himself to jumping of the roof from time to time, only to practice his roll out, readying himself for a hard landing.

During his stay at the hospital, recovering from the plane accident, Jerry met a man called Fred. Fred was in the hospital visiting his wife, who had just undergone surgery. Jerry was very outgoing— people liked him. He liked nothing better than to talk about flying, and most people were impressed by his knowledge. Fred was a crop duster, and operated out of the local airport where Jerry lived.

He took an immediate liking to Jerry, and invited him to go for a ride with him in his biplane someday, with his parent's permission. Jerry told his parents of the offer. They agreed that sometime after he was completely healed he would be allowed to go up with Fred, and only after he had been properly introduced to them.

It was not until after Jerry's eighth birthday that he was allowed to go with his parents to Fred's hanger, and a ride in the biplane. This was to be

Jerry's best birthday present ever. He reasoned it was worth all the pain he suffered during his accident, to end up in the hospital so he could meet Fred. This was what it was all about, moving closer to a real airplane, touching it and actually going up in it. If there was ever a microcosmic doubt about becoming a pilot, and flying airplanes, it had vanished the moment the engine started.

The sound of the motor, the vibration and the power that eased the plane forward, was etched indelibly in his young mind. He could never be anything but a pilot. He had become "one" with the airplane and he felt its freedom. He smelled its fumes, and his heart raced towards the sky.

Though the flight only lasted about 20 minutes his soul never touched down. The spirit can never be grounded, and a flyer must always return to the sky to be one with the soul.

Jerry never slept that night, and for many nights after. He floated around the house in a mindless stupor for days, and could not concentrate on his school work. Over the next few months, and indeed for the next two years, Fred taught him most things Jerry now knows about flying.

The two families became very good friends. Jerry began working part time after school in the hanger. He not only had regular flying lessons, but earned some small change as well. Jerry was liked by most people at the airport, and he could go up with just about anyone he wanted. Because he was a dedicated worker, his services were in demand around the hangers, doing small jobs and clean-ups.

Shortly after Jerry turned 12, Fred announced that he was going to retire and would be moving into the city. His wife needed constant medical attention, and they wanted to be near the hospital. Jerry did not talk to anyone for almost a week. He had always thought Fred would help him with his flying lessons when he got old enough. Now that was all over. He understood and accepted that his dad   didn't make enough money to pay for lessons, and what Jerry earned had been going to his mother. He was heart broken.

Time heals all things, and Jerry moved on. He would still find a way to get his lessons. He thought. Fred had been a good instructor and as young as Jerry was, he could already fly. The only things he did not have now were his pilot's license and a job. He continued working at the airport, with the other pilots and mechanics. They all found work for him to do, and every nickel went to his mom. By his 16th birthday, Jerry had managed to alienate himself from most of his schoolmates. They were tired of listening to him rave on about flying and airplanes. He had earned the nickname of "Flyboy." At first this was a compliment, but later the name was used to make fun of him. He had friends at the hangers, and did not miss the immature talk of the schoolyard.

Jerry now 16 years old had another goal. Like most young people his driver's license was of great significance. A licence meant more freedom, and more responsibility at the hanger, which meant more money. At last he would be able to start saving money for his pilot's licence. Getting the driver's licence was a breeze for him; he had been driving around the airport for the last three years. He was sometimes even allowed to drive the road when it was determined there were no police around.

Jerry was offered a steady job after school and weekends, running errands and doing small mechanical repairs. With the job came an hourly wage, and some flying lessons thrown in, including twin engine flying.

All was going well for Jerry. It seemed like nothing could go wrong. Everything to this point had manifested, as though it had been mapped out before his birth. He would not have to rely on his father to send him to flight school, nor would he have to pay for training. He could take his test now and pass.

The day had arrived for Jerry to go into town to take his driver's exam. His dad rounded up the family into the truck, and off they drove to town. There was a celebration planned after the exam at the local drive-in.

On the way to town his dad had developed severe chest pains, and he could no longer drive. Jerry took over the wheel and raced the truck to the hospital.

His dad had suffered a heart attack, which left him partially paralyzed. He could no longer work on the farms, and spent months recovering. Meanwhile, Jerry's mother took on a cooking job at the drive-in, and Jerry helped support the family with money he earned at the airport. Any money that he had saved for flying lessons was used to help support the family.

For the next two years, Jerry finished his schooling and graduated. He took care of his father after school, and found time to work at the airfield on weekends. There had been few flying lessons since the heart attack, and now no money left for the pilot's licence.

Jerry felt it all slipping away from him. He had to work at holding onto the dream. There was nothing else for him, nothing he wanted to do. His destiny was always clear. For as far back as he could remember, he had to fly. He had to join once again with the sky to reclaim his spirit, and he would not be grounded.

Months later, Jerry said goodbye to his parents. He left home to sign up with the Canadian Air Force, so that he would continue to receive more training and pick up his licence. After three years in the Force he had qualified to fly jets. Jerry had saved some money, and hoped to get a job flying for a small company, until he could afford to upgrade his licence. His aspiration was to fly jumbo jets for a major airline, and he would have nothing else.

On a stopover at an airbase in Ontario, Jerry chanced by a local mall. He was attracted by a large outdoor display which included a scaled down model of a 747. He recognized the man standing in front of the display, in a pilot's uniform. It was one of the pilots, Archie, from the hanger. Jerry had done many odd jobs for him. He walked over to him, and they greeted each other as long lost brothers.

Archie introduced a young lady standing beside him, in a stewardesses uniform, as his daughter Amanda. She was about the same age as Jerry and she was very beautiful, it was love at first sight for Jerry. His heart thundered in his chest and was about to take flight. Amanda had been working for the airline for the last two years, and had been favouring international flights.

Jerry and Amanda got to know each other very well in the next two days, and were extremely attracted to each other. They arranged to meet again when their schedules could be coordinated. Before Jerry left Ontario, Archie suggested that he stop into his office next time he was in town to meet his boss, who always kept his eye open for a good pilot.

Jerry never did go back to Ontario or get a job with the airline; on the other hand, he did keep in touch with Amanda. Their calls became more frequent and, finally after several stopovers in Vancouver they decided that Amanda would move out to British Columbia and they would be married.

Jerry was flying for a small commercial airline, and carrying passengers between Vancouver and Calgary. He had moved into an apartment near the Vancouver airport, and spent most of his time in the air.

Amanda quit her job at the airline she was working for, and got a new job flying out of Vancouver on transcontinental flights. They were married, and a year later Jerry, Amanda and baby moved to a neighbouring community, where they settled into their new house.

Jerry finally got his big break. On June 11, 1985, he received a call from a major airline requesting him to come in for an interview. His friend, and now father-in-law, Archie had transferred to another airline and had highly recommended Jerry for a upcoming position, as captain of a "747 Jumbo Jet." Within a few months, Jerry had realized his life's desire, and was flying jumbo jets on international flights.

Jerry's life was already mapped out before he was born and it was predestined, it seemed, that he would be a pilot. All the circumstances of his life lead him to believe that, and manifest that belief into his experience.

Chapter 2

The Story of Harvey Wong

In the winter of 2001 I took a job with a contracting company, as a heating inspector. The subcontracting company had a contract with a major department store. The job title was just a fancy name for outside salesperson.

It was my responsibility, as an inspector, to go into people's homes and do visual inspections of their heating equipment and ducting systems. Should I notice a need for one of our services, I was to inform the customer, and sell them the service.

On my first day in the office I was given a tour of the building. In the sales office I noticed a large white board. On the board were listed six names, followed by a table with figures in the cells. This was the inspector's totals for the pay period. I noticed at the top of the column the largest figure in dollars and a name beside it—Harvey Wong.

Harvey Wong has been number one in sales consistently, since I have been there which is 42 months at the time of this writing. As part of my learning, I went out with another inspector to get a feel for the job. It was required by most of the inspectors to take someone out, so that they could see the different sales techniques. I didn't go out with Harvey until I had worked there for a year. Harvey did not like taking new inspectors out on leads. Many of his customers were Chinese, and there would be little value in going out with him.

Harvey allowed me to go out with him on one of my days off. During my second year, I became closer to Harvey, and I consider him a friend. Everybody likes Harvey—he is a very positive person, he has that aura about him—he makes friends instantly.

I knew that I would learn from him, and it would enhance my selling abilities.

On our first call Harvey immediately befriended the customer. By the time we got down to the basement, he had already established a good rapport with him. He joked about things, and made positive remarks about the customer's home and about the people he talked with. The observations that I made about Harvey's sales techniques were not something I would use in a sales meeting, or as a presentation to other sales people. His presentations were hurried and lacking in detail. I do not believe that I would buy anything from him if he had come to my door.

Harvey's technique is simple and straightforward. People like Harvey. I do not believe they understand too much of what he is talking about, but they buy from him anyway, because they trust him. Harvey loves what he does, and customers notice that.

Something else t I have noticed about Harvey, is that he makes his own luck. I do not believe in luck or coincidence, so I will rephrase it to say that Harvey creates or manifests circumstances and opportunities that will bring to him the desired results.

Harvey sells most of the leads that come to him; his selling ratio is very high. While other inspectors are struggling to sell their leads, which may be of poor quality, Harvey has somehow managed to gather less leads, but they are all of good quality and he sells them.

He has been with the company for eight years and, of course, he will get referrals. Harvey gets more referrals than anyone else. People tell their friends about Harvey and they, in turn, ask for him. Harvey gives back and tries to help people. He has a wonderful philosophy about helping, "give now and it will come back to you tenfold." Harvey manifests well. He understands that when he helps someone else he is really helping himself.

Being in a position of helping often puts you into situations of being used. Harvey does not let that concern him. Any loses he may incur are all returned to him from other sources. If Harvey lends someone $20 and it is not repaid, he will get an extra lead or make an extra sale that more than compensates him. It always comes back to Harvey, and he knows it. I have never heard Harvey complain, or turn his back on someone because they owe him. He does not expect a return because he knows he will get it. That is the "Great Secret," in manifesting, it is all about knowing.

Harvey was born in Macao China, 57 years ago, and started school there. Like many Chinese men, his father moved to Hong Kong to look for work

and send money back to his family. He took
Harvey, his favourite son, with him. Harvey's
father had three wives and a mistress, and
produced 17 offspring.

Harvey finished most of his junior high in Hong
Kong before moving to Australia at around the age
of fourteen. He finished high school and attended
university for three years. None of the other
children of his father's marriages were sent to
college. Harvey and his dad were very close and he
was well favoured. While in Australia and
attending university, Harvey worked in the labs of
Schweppes.

When he got a call that his dad was sick and
dying of cancer, he returned to Hong Kong at his
dad's request, to be there when he died. His dad
died three years later. Harvey found a job with a
major bank and became one of the best
employees. Shortly after, he was offered a job with
the world's biggest bank, BankAmerica, and took
the position of "loans manager." Traditionally
employees work long hours, but only got paid for
the regular day. Harvey said, "I won't kiss ass,"
which is expected in Hong Kong culture, and he
was subsequently fired.

On a visit to one of his sisters in Calgary,
Alberta, Canada, Harvey fell in love with the
country and applied for landed immigrant status,
then left for Hong Kong, again, for the required
blood test. After three extensions he finally moved
to British Columbia, Canada. Getting a job in BC
was not as easy as he thought. The banks that he
applied to said he was over-qualified for the

positions available, and would not hire him. He applied to a major credit company for a position, and was told he would be contacted by the manager the following Sunday. Harvey told himself that this was the last chance. If he was not hired he would return to Hong Kong, and resume his life there.

Harvey got the phone call he was waiting for, and started working for the company. He sent for his wife in Hong Kong, who was working for an airline. She applied to a bank here and got a position. Harvey made friends with her boss, and was well liked by most of the senior staff. He was asked to join the bank, and agreed.

He was offered another job with a different bank, which he accepted. He was very quickly promoted, and moved to Edmonton. Harvey worked at the bank for the next five or six years and when the government privatized their liquor stores, Harvey bought two of them. Shortly afterwards, he moved his family to BC and settled here. He commuted back and forth for several months, and when he finally tired of traveling, he landed a local job as a heating inspector/salesman. Harvey has worked at this job for several years now, and it is here that I met him.

Harvey considers himself a very successful person. He has always received what he wanted. He does say that his expectations are not high, and he just wants to be comfortable. That is the position he is in now. He has a wife and three children. He lives in a comfortable home and has his two businesses. Harvey works three or four hours a day, then goes to the pub for a couple of beers. He helps his neighbours with their yards on the weekends. He sends money to his mother, now 84 years old, in Edmonton. She lives in a care home, and gives Harvey's money away. It runs in the family!

Harvey lost his son Gerald, a Down's syndrome child, just over a year ago. Gerald was his favourite son. Harvey misses him very much and often visits his grave to talk to him. Harvey believes that Gerald is watching over him, and brings him good luck. He says he has only one regret concerning an old friend, and there is nothing about his past he would change. Harvey wanted "comfortable" and that is what he has manifested. He does not worry, because there is nothing to worry about. He believes his life has purpose, and he lives it with gratitude.

"Don't worry about what you can change, because once you change it, you don't have to worry about it. And don't worry about what you can't change, because worrying won't change it."

Jewish proverb

Chapter 3

> *The story of Vicky is difficult for me to tell, without including myself. I have known Vicky for the last two years, and she is now my significant other. We have been living together for a year. I have the advantage and best opportunity to observe her, and the way she creates the events in her life first hand. The events that I will describe in this chapter will be those that have occurred in her recent history, for the time that I have known her.*
> *(2001-2006)*

Vicky's Story

Vicky is one of the most successful conscious manifestors I have ever known. We all are great manifestors, but most all of us manifest solely on a subconscious level, automatically. We sometimes get what we want, and are frustrated when we do not. That is because we do not understand how the system works. Vicky most often gets what she wants, because she understands how the system works, and she gives it little thought. It is that simple for her.

If Vicky wants something she simply knows that she will get it. Vicky is consciously aware of how the system works, and she does not get in the way of the process. I believe this is one of the most important reasons for her success.

I met Vicky on June 13, 2001, in a meeting I attended with my business partner at his home. Vicky had a promotional idea that was relevant to our business, and wanted to make a pitch to us at this meeting. My partner had met Vicky at his place of work. He is a golf teacher, and Vicky had come for lessons. Her father often practiced at this particular driving range. When I met her, Vicky had only been in Canada for a short time from Singapore. My partner had been dating Vicky for two months, and ended the relationship abruptly, in the summer of 2001. They still maintained a speaking relationship, and Vicky would call him from time to time.

Vicky was in the process of finding a job and wanted to stay in Canada. She had just lost her fiancé to leukemia, before Christmas and was still in the mourning process. It was a time of great sorrow and vulnerability. The break up with my business partner was not supportive of all the feelings she was going through at that time. She had to face a new country, a new career, the death of her fiancé, and the break-up of a recent relationship.

Vicky is 23 years younger than I am. Although she was born in China, she speaks fluent English. I found her to be very attractive and imagined what it would be like to have a relationship with her. I was not looking for a relationship at that time, and it had been two years since I last dated.

I was very comfortable on my own, so I quickly dismissed those thoughts.

After the meeting, it would be another two weeks before I would meet Vicky again. At that time in my life I was semi retired and I spent considerable time at the library. By chance, one day I was working at the computer and looked up to notice Vicky sitting at a large table in the reading area. She seemed really involved in her paper work, so I thought it best that I not disturb her. After several moments had passed, I could not get away from the feeling that I should really go over and say hello just to be friendly.

I casually wondered over to her table and got her attention.

Vicky was in the process of reviewing her new job-related materials. She had finally made a decision between three job offers, and decided to go with a national insurance company as a district rep. I was happy that something positive was working in her life. After patiently listening for a few moments I told her that I had to get back to my computer. I was about to leave, when she suggested she would move over to where I was sitting. Although I really wanted to finish what I was doing, I felt that she wanted to talk some more, so I moved away from the computer and we sat down to chat.

We talked for more than three hours, unaware of the passage of time, until the library closed.

For most of the conversation centered on my writing and what I was doing spiritually. She was very interested in my work, and had some of the same thoughts I had.

As a result of our conversation, Vicky suggested we start up a group in the library to talk about spiritual issues.

I was blown away by this suggestion. I had just finished reading a book on Wisdom Circles a few days before, and thought that it would be a great idea to start up my own circle. Not knowing where to start, I decided that I would leave it for now. I believed an opportunity would present itself when the time was right. This was an amazing coincidence.

We met at the library a week later to talk more about the idea.

A hot July afternoon found many people inside the library, taking advantage of the air conditioning. Vicky and I started talking about what we wanted for the Wisdom Circle, and the criteria we would use to operate it. I remembered a gentleman I had met a couple of weeks earlier, and thought he might be interested in joining the group. I did not know his last name or his phone number but I was sure I would bump into him around town, in the future. For now, I was being selfish and wanted to spend time with Vicky. It was only minutes later that this gentleman walked into the library, and came directly over to our table.

In the course of telling him what we were doing, he asked to be included in the group. He joined in on the discussions and ideas began bouncing back and forth between us.

We must have been talking too loudly. A young man presented himself to our table, and said he overheard us. He was doing a thesis on religion and asked if he could join in. In a period of just two hours, we had already gathered four members. We settled on a regularly-scheduled meeting date, to be held Saturday afternoons, at the library.

During our first meeting, the woman who tends to the flowers overheard us while she was watering them and asked to join. Other people have introduced themselves to us in the similar fashion. All of them put themselves in the right time and place for this circle to be formed.

Vicky brought the appropriate people into her life, at a time when she needed support and friendship. Although these seemed like chance meetings, looking back I can easily see how it was all set up. All of us needed something at that time, and we made ourselves available to get involved in a group that would fulfill those needs. Although the group was formed as a wisdom circle to deal with spiritual ideas, we have bonded and supported each other for three years now.

During our early days with the wisdom circle, Vicky and I dated and formed a close relationship. Because of the nature of her job, she managed her schedule around having time together. There were very few days that we did not see each other.

During the time of Vicky's arrival in my life, I had spent the previous 13 years in a close relationship with my stepson. We had spent all those years doing things together, and often travelled to play golf. Just before his 14th birthday, he started excluding me from his life. He was entering into his first days of puberty, and his right of ascension into manhood. He cut off all contact with me for more than a year.

The timing for him to do this was in harmony with the current events that were unfolding in my life. I needed to develop my relationship with Vicky, and his actions gave us that opportunity. He wanted time with his friends, away from golf tournaments, practice and me. He used my new relationship with Vicky to facilitate that desire, and it worked for both of us.

Vicky had made up her mind to go back to school and get her MBA degree. She applied to a local university and was immediately accepted. She applied for, and received, her student loan without any complications. She also received a scholarship, and a job as a teaching assistant at the university. All of this fell into place, as if it were predestined. She left her job with the insurance company, and prepared for her courses.

Vicky and I talked about getting married. We decided we would have a small wedding, before the end of the year. With that in mind, we made arrangements to move in together in the summer of 2002.

We looked at apartments, and decided that we should look into townhouses or a co-op. That way we could get involved, and develop new friendships as a couple. She searched the web and downloaded several applications. Vicky filled them out and mailed them back. A week later, we got a call to have an orientation meeting in a co-op that was located in the same community as the University she would be attending in the fall. Five couples had applied for the only available unit, and we were chosen. The location was perfect, it was only 15 minutes to campus, and exactly 15 minutes from my job. The setting was ideal for the lifestyle that we would maintain for the next two years.

We did not know where Vicky would be working when she finished her course, we expected it would be out of the country. Since we assumed we would be travelling, we decided not to spend too much on furnishings. Within a month of moving into our place, we had found everything we needed at garage sales. We passed by hundreds of garage sales. At those we did stop into, we found exactly what we wanted, and saved a great deal of money.

Our plans were to be married before Christmas. A week after Vicky and I had made the decision to get married, my estranged wife called me up and suggested that we should finally file for divorce. I had already purchased a kit to do it myself, several years earlier, and I gave it to her to do the paper work. She and a friend filled out the forms but never finished. I suggested I would do it myself, and retrieved the paperwork.

To make a long story short, the paperwork was done incorrectly so I redid it and filed it myself. Because of a mistake in the paperwork regarding filing procedures the court never processed the documents. My divorce did not go through until the end of January. Everything, up to this date, worked perfectly, but there were things standing in the way of our upcoming marriage. From the beginning, it became more apparent that Vicky and I were putting up roadblocks to the marriage. We enjoyed being together and missed each other's presence when we were not. But we did not want to make the commitment to be married, and we were manifesting obstacles at every turn.

We have dealt with most of the issues that surrounded our relationship, age difference, ethnic differences, and family blessings. But we did not deal with the real issue of why we wanted to get married, so we manifested subconsciously different elements that would postpone the marriage. We loved each other, and liked doing things together. Marriage always seemed to be in the future, and a natural course of events.

When I first started my job, I was working afternoons, which was great because Vicky's appointments were mostly in the early evenings, giving us time to spend together. Vicky quit her job, started school, and her evenings opened up. Shortly after this change, my boss called me into the office and said that he was taking me off afternoons and putting me on day shift. This left my evenings free, and more time to spend with Vicky—it all worked out perfectly.

Once again circumstances were created that would allow us more time together. Still we do not know yet why the marriage was in a constant state of postponement.

For the first nine months on my job, I was driving a full size van on my leads and it was becoming very expensive, with gas and repairs. I mentioned to Vicky that I should really get a smaller car and she asked me what I wanted. I knew I wanted a Japanese car, and since I was not familiar with the models, I struggled to come up with a name. I remembered, just the day before I was following an Acura, so I blurted out, an Acura. She asked me what colour and I said it did not matter. Somewhat irritated, she announced that she needed something to work with, so I said forest green. She asked, "how about red?" I said great, that red would be perfect.

Two weeks had passed, when one day she called me on the phone from work, very excited. At the building where she worked, she had found a private ad on the bulletin board, with a picture of a red Acura for sale.

Not wasting any time after work, we drove to the city to see the car. A wonderful opportunity presented itself. The car looked like brand-new and in mint condition with unusually low kilometres. We took the car out for a road test. When we returned, we told the woman we would take it. We also told her we had to sell my van first because I did not have all the cash. I asked her what she wanted for a deposit. She said that a deposit was not necessary—our word was good enough.

The woman said she would hold the car for three weeks. It had to be moved by then as the house was sold and the family would be moving. Vicky had recently received a sum of money. She asked me if she could lend me the money for the car until I sold my van and I agreed.

The car was exactly what Vicky had envisioned when I had told her that I was thinking of buying another car. The only exception was I said I wanted four doors and the car we just bought was a two-door model. This is such a great story I tell it whenever I can.

A letter arrived from the university informing Vicky that she had been nominated for a fellowship. This meant that she did not have to work as a teaching assistant this fall, and could devote all her time to studying.

As I mentioned earlier, Vicky and I thought that we would be moving to another country after her graduation. She had to do a three-month internship in the summer, locally, after which the job hunting would begin in earnest.

There were several positions available for the internship, and only one locally in Vancouver. Of course, most all the students wanted the local position. Some of them had families and did not want to travel. The companies that sponsored the courses interviewed all the students and internships assigned. A local company was the last to do the interviewing, and Vicky landed the position.

During the interview with the company Vicky was informed of her salary for the three months of the internship. When she accepted the job, the salary turned out to be double what she expected.

Over the last six weeks, my sales at work had been declining as we moved into the slow time of the year. On two separate occasions, my boss called me to the office. There was little chance of me remaining on the job if my sales did not increase, and looking over the sales leads I was getting, one would easily conclude that it was mostly bad luck.

The truth is I had been losing interest in the job for some time, and it would have been only a short time before I would be asked to leave. What I really wanted to do was to write my books and articles

The news of Vicky's doubled salary was timely. Extra money was now available to run the household, while I took the summer off to write. Vicky volunteered to put the extra cash into our account for this purpose. She, once again, opened a door for me, and I went through it. I completed three books in the four weeks that I had been off work.

I asked Vicky to represent me as my literary agent for my second book, and she agreed. Neither one of us has had any experience in publishing, and we wanted to do this ourselves.

Vicky was born in Hong Kong. She was a sickly child with asthma, and was cared for by a maid during her younger years. She was not allowed to play with the other kids because of her condition and eventually withdrew inside herself. She had very few social skills and, as she grew up, she stayed away from people out of fear.

Vicky's father was a math teacher, and her mother worked as a secretary. They eventually opened up a stationary store, and expanded to two. Vicky helped at the store after school, but spent most of her time studying in the stock room. She did not know how to interact with the customers, so she spent a lot of her time starring out the window onto the street below. For much of her childhood, the memories are blurred.

Vicky graduated from high school in Hong Kong. Her first taste of independence came when she attended college at St. Cloud State University in Minnesota USA, and then at the University of Minnesota. She chose math because her English skills were not fully developed yet, and she did not have to talk as much in a math course. Gradually, her classmates assimilated her into the school culture and she began to emerge from her shell to become a social butterfly—no longer willing to sit at the window and watch life pass her by.

Vicky returned to Hong Kong, and stayed with her parents after her graduation. She secured at a job with an actuarial consulting company in Hong Kong, and was transferred to Singapore. A job offer in Singapore with another company allowed her to stay there for seven years. During this time, she met someone and fell in love. He proposed marriage and they were engaged. He was sick at the time and Vicky nursed him through treatment for leukemia. Three months later he died.

Vicky visited her parents in British Columbia, Canada, in 2001 shortly after his death. I met Vicky while she was visiting her folks, and we started dating.

We now have a committed relationship, and live together in a small city just outside of Vancouver. Although Vicky and I proposed marriage, we agreed to wait for a while and move in together first. We have based our new relationship on personal growth and development, and that will be our focus.

Every day Vicky continues to amaze me. She creates so easily, consciously and subconsciously, all the things that she desires in her life. If you were to ask her what her secret is, she will tell you that you must know what you want, it must be purposeful and you must know you have it already. This knowledge has led her to successful manifesting, and has all the essential elements that make it work. She is a living testament as to how effectively the system works, and can work for anyone on a conscious level. If Vicky can have anything she desires, and create it effortlessly—so can I, and anyone else.

Chapter 4

A Little About Roy

I am going to include some of my own profile from the past three years and a brief summary of earlier times. As far as I am concerned, it has been only the last three years that I have actively been aware of whom I am, and it will always be an ongoing process. Some of what I am going to tell you, I have never told anyone. I have kept secret some of my life's experiences of four years ago, so do not tell anybody.

My ego is going to have difficulty with what I am going to write. In the best interests of the reader, what you are going to read in the next few chapters will give you a greater insight into how I have manifested some of the circumstances of my life. You may be able to relate to some of it.

Four years ago, I was involved with my own business of 15 years. It was a small, successful storefront operation with sales of over $300,000 per annum. This is a good business for a one-man turnkey operation. I sold off parts of my company because I could not handle the work myself, and had difficulty getting reliable help. I built my business in a modular style so that any part of it could be operated independently of the other, as a separate operation.

I worked by myself, with only occasional part time help in the last three years I was in operation. I believed I could not get responsible help, and that was the kind of help I attracted most of the time. I made myself indispensable, and found myself working seven days a week, with ten hours being a short day.

I always had money in my pocket and owned an expensive motor home, travelled, and thought little about spending money on anything that I wanted. My family and friends were recipients of my generosity. I lived alone and liked it. My second wife and I had been separated for almost 20 years, yet I still had contact with her and the stepchildren and I helped support the youngest one that was living at home.

My oldest stepson gave me a book, "The Way of the Peaceful Warrior," by Dan Millman. That book was the beginning of a change in the way I was living.

I read few books since I finished school, except for the computer books I needed to run the business. I asked my son if he had any other books and he brought me, "Conversations with God, Book One," by, Neale Donald Walsch. I was so impressed with this book; I bought his next one, and have now read all of his works several times.

The books came at an important crossroads in my life, and I could feel the winds of change as I was beginning to look for something more. I had all the physical possessions I really wanted, and I was puzzled by the sudden desire to rid myself of them. I ended a long time relationship with my girlfriend, and was content to be on my own.

In my last year of business I was so burned out that sometimes I would not answer the phone. My store was very busy, and I seldom had lunch, and I never took a break. I decided to get out of the business and do it very quickly. I put an ad in the paper with a selling price of *zero dollars* for the business. I was willing to give the it away just to get out. Two weeks later the only response I had to the ad was from a caller who wanted to know what was wrong with it. I Obviously was not asking enough money.

I closed the doors and sent all the store fixtures to auction. I had a garage sale at the store for some of the tools and other items. The stock was put into storage, and sold later. I paid off most of the suppliers, and declared personal bankruptcy. The business remained untouched—I took the hit personally. I sold almost everything that I owned. Getting out was the most important thing to do, so I sold everything I owned. I wanted to get away from money and business issues, and concentrate on the spiritual side of life. I got what I wanted and ended up with nothing, believing that this is what I had to do to be enlightened

I started to collect books on the subject of spirituality and I began to practice meditation again. I began writing articles to send out for publication in newspapers, and started the wisdom circle in the local library.

With some money saved, and some people owed me money, I survived for a short time at the townhouse I lived in, and then finally moved into my van. I rented a storage locker and setup a small office there. Money was slow coming in, and at times I skipped meals. I literally manifested exactly what I said I wanted—I did not want to have to worry about money. Now I had no money to worry about. There was always just enough to keep me alive and little else. When the money reached zero, I would manage to land a small job that would keep me going for a while, but not enough to put anything away for a rainy day.

During the first year I did not look for work. I helped some friends that owned a local restaurant, working for only food, and they allowed me to keep the tips. I really liked the job, and I met some great people. However, I set myself up to be taken advantage of, and eventually I was expected to take care of the couple's young daughter. I am not sure how I manifested that one. I ended the relationship quickly by refusing to do it, and I lost the couple as friends. It was a great opportunity for me to be immersed in the Chinese culture, and it was another step that would lead me to a relationship with Vicky.

In February of 2001, I started taking notice of stories about guardian angels. I had been to a spiritualist and was introduced to my own spirit guides. I was hooked and one night I prayed for my own guardian angel. The image I had, and looked for, was one of an older man with beard, white hair and wisdom surrounding him.

I started to notice men that were appearing with regularity in places that I frequented. I never made contact with any of them, nor did they notice me. I did not understand what the procedure was, or if there was a procedure. One or two of these men, were showing up consistently in places I went to, even other cities. I thought I was on the right track. I was somewhat bewildered by the events, I had manifested the people in my life that were to help me, and I was not being noticed. I was not about to go up to strangers and tap them on the shoulder and ask if they were my guardian angel.

After a month or so I gave up, or forgot about getting a guardian angel. In any event, I stopped looking for grey-haired strangers.

My story really starts shortly after I met Vicky. We started dating just after we organized the wisdom circle, and the time we spent together was taken up with talks about spirituality and what it meant to us. I never talked to Vicky about wanting, or looking for a guardian angel.

One evening while we were cuddled together, she turned to me and whispered in my ear, "Roy, "I'm your guardian angel." It took me off guard, and I was speechless, I could only listen to her repeat herself. I had no reason to disbelieve what she was saying. Her words came naturally and I totally accepted what she said. She was not exactly what I was looking for in an angel, but I knew straight away she was what she claimed, and I still believe it after almost two years with her.

If you have read the story about the fisherman and the Star Maiden, you will remember that the fisherman, after years of marriage and success in his business, finally looked into the basket that the maiden brought with her into the relationship, even after stern warnings of what would happen if he did. His curiosity got the better of him, he looked and saw nothing, he laughed to himself. He did not see the obvious, the love that was there. When the maiden learned of this violation, she left him, and his business failed once more. When I looked into the basket that Vicky brought with her, I saw the love, but I did not see angel stuff or wisdom, any magic or divine messages, no angel dust.

I spent some time looking into the basket before I saw the truth or wisdom of why she was here. I did not need her to give me anything. I had all that I needed. I had the wisdom already within me. Vicky was sent to me, to challenge me to use it. I got my angel, not in the way I supposed, in the way that I needed. Many times, she is just a pain in the butt and I bless her for that every day. Each of those times, she is bringing a gift to me—if only I would recognize it. She brings me the opportunity, to manifest what it is that I desire at the time. I do not like it when she challenges me, but I recognize the opportunity that she brings and I am grateful that I looked into the basket and saw the gift.

The love that I felt for Vicky, inspired me to manifest my very first book, called Star Maiden, it is not finished yet.

In the past I have not regarded myself as a positive person, and I have viewed my manifesting as poor quality. My root thought has always been that it cannot last, something will happen or I am unworthy. Most of the time I am correct, and I always get what I think about. It has been hard to see the light except in hindsight.

A case in point; at my job I am involved in outside sales I am usually given six leads a day. On this particular day, I was given only two. I was $300 short for the pay period to get to my next level of commission, which meant an extra bonus of $160 on my paycheque. I sold one out of the two, which put me only $30 short of the next level. I was determined to sell something else, even if it meant I had to buy something myself. I returned to the office to do some cold calling on the phone.

As I pulled into the parking lot, I received a call from the office with another lead. I went to the call and sold it. "Great," I thought "I was now over and into the next level." I received a call from another salesman—he gave me one of his leads that he didn't have time to do, and I sold that one as well. This was all before lunch. I picked up more leads and sold them. I then moved into the next higher sales commission bracket. I could not believe my luck, (remember that last line.) I thought now, "All I need to have, are cancellations when I get back to the office."

When I did return to the office, one scheduled appointment had re-scheduled into the following week and out of the current pay period. Well, "I thought that's OK, I'm away up as long as nothing else happens." I went home feeling very good and hoping that there would be no cancellation slips in my bin in the morning. I received a call at home that a customer had cancelled.

As you may have guessed, when I arrived at the office in the morning my worst fears were realized. So many had cancelled, or rescheduled, that I was down into the lowest level for commissions. I could not sustain my good fortune, because my root thought was that *it was too good to be true.* A perfect day of manifesting great sales turned into a not so good day of manifesting cancellations. *"This is the way it always happens,"* I thought, and of course, I was correct.

In the fall of 2002, there were many breakdowns in equipment, lots of mishandling of appointments at the office, and other considerations. The fall is the time of year when we make our living. It just did not happen, and I became very discouraged. Since then, I have not tried very hard, and some of the problems continued. I am a very good sales person, however I started drawing poor quality leads, I did not recover from the disaster of the fall and my sales have started showing it.

My leads dropped in half from the previous year and I have fewer sales. I was called into the office twice about it. During this time, I had given much thought about writing—I had ideas for at least four books I wanted to write, now. It wasn't long before the office would terminate me.

Vicky's job has given her double the wage she was expecting, and she suggested I take the summer off and write. Her salary would more than cover the expenses at home. I agreed and, as of now have written two books and am more than halfway through my third. I have lots of time to manage my web site and write ebooks. In hindsight only, I can see how I manifested this opportunity. It is now easy to see how all the events that were going on in my life over the last few months, were in preparation for me having the time to write. Even during the first two weeks that I had away from the job, I was thinking about how unlucky I was, until the light came on. Bingo, I got what I wanted.

There is only one element missing from what I have manifested—I wanted to be able to contribute to the maintenance of the household at the same time. This element probably has a lot to do with what Vicky wanted to experience. I did not consider it in my assessment of the recent events. My ego was lost in its own considerations. Of course, there is more than me involved in this manifestation.

The realization now is that writing is a full time job. Should I have done well on the job and stayed with it over the summer, there would not have been enough time to complete my books. I got what I wanted, but I was hung up on the details. It happened in spite of how I thought it should work.

In the two and a half weeks following my leaving my job, new ideas were coming so fast that I did not find the time to write them all down, and I forgot many of them. The truth was, I was manifesting so quickly that I do not see the trees for the forest.

Now, I am able to spend much of my time talking, teaching and writing about manifesting. Sometimes, I have missed the "Great Secret."

Nothing happens by accident, and the things I have viewed as being negatively manifested, are elements in my life that are bringing the best opportunities to me. They lead to the next step of bringing to me the things that I desire most. The remnants of a root thought that I have about being successful, is the only thought that stands between me and the things that I desire. I always get what I think about and that is a "Great Truth."

"A man travels the world over in search of what he needs, and returns home to find it."[16]

---

[16] George Moore

Chapter 5

Simple Manifesting

Manifesting is the ability to create matter from thought, to create something from nothing. Matter is the manifestation of energy into physical form.

If you are familiar with physics and quantum physics or have read Gary Zukav's book "The Dancing Wu Li Masters," you will know that physical objects are simply thoughts in physical form. All things in the physical world are made of the same stuff. The atoms that make up a tree, a rock or your supper, are the same atoms that you are made of. Scientifically ... every living 'thing' is energy manifesting as that 'thing'. Newton saw his laws as manifestations of God's perfection.

"The duration of an event or object in space or time is determined by the intensity of the thoughts or emotions that gave it birth."[17]

Physical objects are symbols of your thinking. It is cause and effect. Your thought is the cause, and the effect is the manifestation. At some level, whenever you picture something in your mind, you have already created it. The more you focus on the thought, the greater the chances of it coming into your reality. To the degree that it is fervently held as truth, to that degree will it be

---

[17] Jane Roberts, "The Nature of Personal Reality"

made manifest in your experience. If you want to know what is going on in your subconscious, all you have to do is look at the things that are in your life now. Your present experiences, the state of your health and well being, and the physical objects that you have accumulated around you, will demonstrate what's going on in your head, at this moment.

That which you think of, but thereafter never speak of, creates at one level. That which you think of and speak of creates at another
level. That which you think, speak, and do becomes made manifest in your reality.[18]

The three steps in the process of manifesting anything are; thought, word and deed, which correspond to the triune, which is you—mind, spirit and body. The thought is first imagined by the mind, then it is acted upon by the spirit that gives life and the result is the body (the physical world). It always follows in that order and is no more complicated than that—think it, speak it and do it.

To paraphrase the process, first you must create something in your mind, a desire. Then you must speak it with authority, so that the universe knows what it is you desire and then the deed will

_____

[18] Neale Donald Walsch, "Conversations with God Book One"

be done. The second step is the most misunderstood element in manifesting, and many of us try to eliminate this part of the process, yet it is the most powerful of the three steps.

Any word that follows the word "I," must be made so, it is the law of the universe. Speaking it starts the manifesting process and cannot be eliminated. I am happy, I am sad, I am rich, I am poor, I am angry, I am joyful. I will do this I will do that. Say it with authority, say it loud, and say it often. Let everyone know what it is you want.

Often we are not often clear in our thoughts about what it is we desire. When this happens, a conflict between spirit and personality occurs, and free choice or ego always gets what it wants. Most often, it is materialistic and not in harmony with what the spirit wants.

The spirit will patiently wait and create another opportunity, so that the ego may choose the probability the subconscious wishes to experience. As the ego matures, more often it will choose correctly. The more often it chooses what the spirit desires, the closer it gets to enlightenment, until finally it becomes one again with the spirit and melds with that which creates all that is.

If we have not manifested that which is in harmony with the spirit, we either chose not to at some level of consciousness, or we realized that we did not translate the spirit's wishes effectively into words that would manifest the thoughts into the form that we desire. If, for example, I ask for a lot of money because it will make me happy, the result may be a lot of money, but I may not get what I really want, the happiness that I desired. Had I asked for happiness, I may not get the money because the root thought is the happiness, and I do not need money to be happy. I need to examine the rationale for believing that money will make me happy, and I must be specific when I ask for it.

"If all your beliefs, not just your "fortunate" ones, were not materialized, you would never thoroughly understand on a physical level that your ideas create reality."[19]

The universe follows natural laws that are irrefutable and cannot be changed. The universe is impersonal, and must follow the law—it does not work for some and not others because of who you are, or how you may have manifested your life. It works equally well for all those who know how to use it. When you think of something, it has no choice but to act on it, in the way that you have created it. 'Man' is the only manifestation that has the capacity to be co-creator with his/her source. This may be done at any level of your consciousness.

The reason we meditate is so that we may get closer to the subconscious and be attuned or aligned with it and become aware of what it is we really desire at that level, so that we may consciously participate in the manifesting process into physicality. Know always that we will get what

---

[19] Jane Roberts, "The Nature of Personal Reality"

we desire. You must also know that what you know will be so.

To believe in your own weakness or inability to manifest your thoughts into reality, is to deny yourself the power of action. You can do it; you simply need to *know* that you can.

"The film is like the mind, for the mind is the source of patterns. The result is pictures on the screen. The physical manifestation, what we experience, is the result of the patterning of light."[20]

All manifesting must have purpose before it will work. To say that you want a million dollars will not get you a million dollars, if you do not know why you want the million dollars. You cannot fool the universe or yourself, you must be 100% honest with yourself, or you may get something other than what it is you desire.

If again, for example, you asked for a million dollars because you believe that it will make you happy, what you may get is the experience of being happy without the million dollars. On the other hand, you may get the experience of wanting to be happy and feeling unfulfilled because you did not get the million dollars, or you may get the million dollars and still not be happy.

You must be aware of why you are asking for that which you desire. Having not manifested the million dollars, your ego will observe that manifesting does not work even though you

---

[20] Henry Reid, "Edgar Cayce: Channeling Your Higher Self"

always get what you want, whether you know it or not. If you are aware enough you will always experience getting what you desire. If you do not know what the purpose of the manifestation is, you may experience not getting what it is you desired.

There are only two things that each of us does every day, all day long. We create or we remember. We are either creating new things in our mind and manifesting them, or we are remembering old things in our mind and recreating them. There are an average of 65,000 thoughts running through our head every day, and 80% of them are old ideas, old business. We are continually rehashing thoughts that have little or no relevance to our life today. This is the ego's way of reassuring itself of its own existence. It continually lives in a time and place that is known to it.

"When the arrow leaves the bow, it no longer belongs to the archer." The ego hangs on to as many of its arrows as it can. The ego is mistaken. The only thing that is consistent in the universe is change.

If only the ego would let go of the old thoughts, and realize that it is creator in all the new thoughts and creations, it would realize its significance in the relationship with mind and spirit. It would know its importance and that it is the free choice (ego) that enables the spirit to experience in the physical world. It would create its own immortality. It would know itself to be indispensable.

Ego knows its connection to the spirit at some level and it is fear that holds it back. Over time ego has been taught that it is separate from spirit, and it believes it. To give up its autonomy, it fears it would have to give up its existence, to pass into extinction. Life always exists on the edge of comfort. It is the next step past the comfort zone that brings life, brings evolution, and brings eternity.

Between the two choices of remembering and creating, it is where we spend most of our time that brings the desired or undesired manifestations. Controlling our thoughts should be our priority; subsequently we will be able to control our manifesting.

Most adults stop developing their minds at age thirty. We stop learning, stop reading, stop asking questions. Worse, we rely on TV and other media to inform and dictate the circumstances of our life. We are moulded and shaped by our environment and the people around us.

We accept other people's ideas, instead of creating our own. We accept the images we see in magazines and on TV as being truthful. We accept opinions and carefully structured news casts as statements of the way things really are. By accepting these false realities, we manifest them *en masse* into our own experience of truth.

As I wrote in my book, "The New Age of Healing," 98% of our bodies are replaced every year. How it turns out is conditional on what we remember, or wish to create. If we have sickness or an abnormality, it will be re-created each year from memory. If we had cancer last year, we will have it again this year, because we remembered it, it will be recreated from memory that is locked into our DNA.

If we desire healing or change, that is what will be manifested. We must then see ourselves as healthy and that is what we will create. Illness is an error in thought. Illness is an outward manifestation of something that is going on with our thinking.

It is a paradox in that we were given the gift of no memory when we came into this world, so that we would begin to recreate and manifest using our free will. It is our physical memory that gives us the most grief and gets in our way of manifesting what we really desire. It is because we have forgotten who we really are, that we manifest all those things that bringing us unhappiness and discomfort. That was never the way it was meant to be. Life was never meant to be difficult. We make it that way, because somewhere we were told that doing without—suffering was virtuous and that had purpose.

There is no purpose in suffering from lack or sickness, other than the purpose that each of us gives it. Some think that it is to glorify God that we make ourselves humble, weak and subservient—but I see the opposite. If a system were working responsibly and in the best interest of all, would it not glorify God even more to have his children healthy, wealthy and joyous? Would success, peace and joy not glorify him even more? Have we not made ourselves children of a lesser

God, by continuing with the false image of suffering and fear? Have we not manifested a petty God by still believing in this theology?

We have become great manifestors of war, famine, disease and natural disasters. Why do we suffer from this falsehood? It is because we still believe in it. It is still part of our truth. We still manifest wars because we belief that it can be justified. When we say that we do not believe in war, that is all we get back from the universe. Saying that you do not believe in war does not give you peace. It is only when we say that we belief in peace, that we manifest peace. When enough of us believe in peace, we will have peace in the world.

Peace is an individual thing, when you know that you are at peace with yourself, peace is what you will experience.

It is about time that we remembered the mechanics of manifesting, and use it to make our existence, peaceful, loving and fruitful. Practice this approach to manifesting and creating; the awareness will bring you more joy and happiness, and you'll be in control. Do not be against war, be for peace, do not be against killing—be life affirming and do not be against poverty—manifest abundance. Whatever you are against is only a declaration that will not, most often, bring positive results—until you stand for its opposite. When you are against something, you are virtually at war with it. We know that war does not work. It is observable, throughout our history, that war has not brought us peace, it has not brought us what we really want. By being against a thing, you are not demonstrating what you are for, and you are giving it life. Live your truth, demonstrate who you are, and create the opposite of what you are against.

> *"To become stronger, change your thoughts. It's as simple and uncomplicated as that."*[21]

Our brain is no more than a thought processor, a computer that processes sensory information about our surroundings in the physical world. Our mind is not our brain. Our mind is who we believe ourselves to be, it is our ego. Moreover, that mind is an illusion. There is only one mind of which we are all a part of, and it is that mind that is real, it is that which gives us life. Our ego cannot live in the present moment, it is physically impossible. By the time sensory information is processed in our brain, the event has already passed and the brain receives old information. Our ego operates only in the past or the future, and that is why it spends so much time in either place.

Our ego is so fragile; it believes that it is always on the edge of extinction, and that is why we fear death so much. The ego believes it will be non-existent when the body dies. The ego likes familiarity; and it feels more secure and the very thing that the ego treasures mostly, "security," is what threatens it the most.

---

[21] Adam Khan

Major threats to the ego are new ideas and thoughts and unfamiliar philosophy. The ego sits on your left shoulder arguing with the angel on your right shoulder. Your ego tells you that you cannot have a thing, because your ego believes that manifesting is too difficult. It is understood that only those with special powers are blessed or privileged, are more deserving.

It is your ego which, both causes you to desire something, and causes you to know that you cannot have it. You are engaged in a constant tug of war between "can" and "can't."

The truth is that we can have anything we desire. It is in the moment that we say we cannot, that we cannot. It is in the moment we know we have it, that we will have it.

In the story of Harvey Wong, we saw that Harvey attracts opportunity to himself. His personality, and a belief in his skills, sells the services he offers. Harvey is a very positive person and already knows he is successful. He does not worry about not making a sale. For every "one" he does not make, he knows the others will make up for it, or another lead or referral from a customer will come along. Harvey does not work very hard at his job, because he does not have to—most days he only works 3-4 hours. On the days that I ask him how his day was, he says, "You know me, I always sell something."

Harvey may sell more if he worked longer hours. Depending on what his thoughts were about working longer and harder, longer may actually work against him. He would have to be perfectly clear about why he believes he needs to work longer or harder. If he believes he does not have enough money, then that is what he will get back from the universe, not enough money. It does not matter how much more he makes, it will never be enough. If he believes he needs to work longer, then that is what he will get back, and he will be working longer. If he simply has a desire to make more money, then that is what he should be focused on. Our thoughts about why we are doing a thing must be perfectly clear before we will get it.

In the story about Jerry, he knew from the time he was an infant that he would fly, and there was never a doubt about it. He never knew why he wanted to be a pilot, he just knew, "because." At times it seemed things would come up that would destroy his possibilities of getting his wings. For instance, when his father had the heart attack Jerry could have envisioned his whole world collapsing, yet this element in his life was just another step to becoming a pilot. Jerry's thoughts were on his father getting well, and helping to support the family. He never gave up on the idea that he would not be a pilot. From time to time, the path took a different route than anticipated ,but all of the experiences were stepping-stones to becoming a pilot, whether he understood it at the time or not.

It is my belief, and that of the New Age/New Thought movement, that before we are born we choose our parents and the circumstances of our birth. We choose the parents most likely to give us the characteristics and opportunities in the physical life, that will bring forth the desired experience. Free will always has first choice in manifesting. Spirit has patience, and keeps providing us with opportunities for manifesting that which it desires, without interfering in our autonomy.

"To act in an independent manner, you must begin to initiate action that you want to occur physically by creating it in you own being."[22]

Our birth is purposeful and not by accident. After we are born, and for the next three or four years, we begin to forget who we are, and why we have come, in order to let the process of life work. We accept the identity that our parents have given us. We adopt their beliefs and characteristics, and we start to become what they have imagined us to be.

If on the other hand, our parents are at an advanced stage of enlightenment, they will interfere less with our development, and remind us constantly of whom we really are. Enlightened parents would encourage us to be ourselves, to act spontaneously, and to be creative. They will remind us that we have unlimited power. They will guide us in using that power for our better selves and that of the community.

They will remind us of our connection to each other, and our environment. If we have planned our birth well, the circumstances allowing us to

---

[22] Jane Roberts, "The Nature of Personal Reality"

experience what we desired will start to unfold. If we are living in harmony with spirit, we will recognize the opportunities that coming our way, and choose the appropriate one.

From a very early age Jerry knew he wanted to fly, he wanted to be a pilot. It was always apparent and all things led him into becoming a pilot. Yet we cannot say with absolute certainty that it is what he really wanted to experience at a spiritual level. We cannot judge him accurately, because the experience of flying may have led to something else that gave him the opportunity to realize what he chose to experience in his physical life. The choices that would bring about the experience are infinite.

For this reason we cannot judge anyone, since we do not know what it is they want to experience. It may seem obvious to us, but it is judged through human experience, and may not have any relevance to his purpose. We can say with certainty that Jerry manifested a flying career. We can observe that it happened. It may have been only a stepping-stone.

One of the biggest roadblocks to getting that which we desire is that we do not really know what it is that we really want in the first place. We may say that we want money, lots of money because it will make us happy, but is that what we really want. Why are we not happy once we get the money? Why do some people that win large sums of money not find happiness? It is because they did not know what their root thought was before they started trying to manifest money.

Some people do not understand that money does not bring happiness. Being happy first should be the "root," thought, the money would come automatically. When you are happy in your experience, abundance always follows. You will enjoy your money when you do get it. If you are not happy with the process of life, you will not be happy with the results. Seek first to manifest what it is you really desire.

Picture in your mind, for a moment, a man who is very hungry; he has not eaten for the last twenty-four hours. This man has the power to order and pay for what ever he wants in the restaurant.

He places a large order enough to feed four people. Two minutes later, he calls the waiter back, cancels the order, and chooses something else. A minute later, he signals the waiter once again and chooses something else. Before the waiter has a chance to hand in the order, the man changes his mind and adds something else.

The waiter has lost his patience by this time and asks the man to leave. The man did not get what he wanted, which was to have food and to satisfy the craving of hunger. He focused on the details, or process, rather than manifesting an end to his hunger, and he created chaos. Those involved were left with their own judgements about what happened, and no one understood the significance of the experience.

A huge obstacle in manifesting what we desire, is in changing our minds about what it is we want. It is much easier to change our mind, if we do not know what it is we desire in the first place. The fastest way to get somewhere, or have something, is to know you are already there or already have it. If we concentrate too much on details, we will never get there, or have it. It is in truth that those around us will help us manifest our desires. Their energy, added to ours will produce even faster results when they know what we desire. When the people involved do not understand what it is that they want, the result is chaos. Everyone is trying to create something different, and they are interpreting our thoughts incorrectly. If we say we are hungry, without a clear description of what it is we want to eat, we may get porridge instead of sirloin.

If, in your mind, it is your desire to have a brand new "Red Mustang convertible," with all the accessories, then that is what you will manifest. If you start worrying about how to go about getting it, you may not manifest it. Simply know that you will have it, and the opportunity will present itself without your help.

Do not create chaos by trying to tell the universe how to go about manifesting the car, leave it alone. The system of manifesting is so simple that all too often we try to make it more complicated than it needs to be. In the human condition, simplicity is often viewed with much less value, or favour. Know this, "the system works," get out of the way and let it happen!

Quality of thought is important and vital to good quality manifesting. DO NOT ASK FOR SOMETHING, you will not get it. The "Great

Secret," to manifesting is in knowing it is you, who is creating the opportunity to get what you desire. The universe is reflective and subservient to your commands. If you "ask" for something, you are sending the message out that you do not have it. What you will get back is an awareness of lack, and an experience of wanting—you may never get what you want. However, if you desire something, it is a preference. A desire is not a "want," and to desire something does not suggest lack.

My suggestion is to know you already have the thing that you desire, show gratitude for that which is already yours. Gratitude is a confirmation of something that is already a part of your experience.

A former employer of mine has a motto he holds as an irrefutable truth; "Buyers are Liars," and of course, he has never been wrong. For those of us who have ever been in sales, we know from experience that buyers do lie if they are not interested in what you are trying to sell them. It is easy to see how that truism came about. However, by believing in this motto one sets oneself up to receive liars into their life. By prejudging his customers as liars, he always manifests liars in his experience.

A major problem with believing in liars is that it carries over into all segments of his life. My ex-boss brings people who lie to him in his business, daily. He surrounds himself with people who lie. The greater the lie, and the more money these people want, the greater the value he places on them—he always ends up on the loosing end of the deal. He appears to place little value on good advice, and significantly more on expensive, unqualified, bad advice. The results are always observable, he does not get what he wants, and he repeats the same mistake time and time again. He has become an expert in manifesting the same circumstances, leading to stagnation in his personal and business development. His business is on a roller coaster ride that always leads back to the same place.

One of the best ways of always being right is to believe it. The ego finds asylum in repeating its mistakes. To the ego, making familiar mistakes is always preferable to any kind of change that might lead to its extinction.

Vicky is very successful at manifesting, because she knows what it is she desires, and its purpose. She has always had money, because she likes to spend it. She is successful, because she likes to be successful. Her intentions are clear to her, and reflected in the quality of her manifestations.

Ask a small child why they did something, and they will tell you "because." Have you ever heard that one? It is probably the most honest answer that you could expect from a child who did something without obvious purpose. They do not need a reason to do it. They did it "because." It is only an adult who would demand a more complex answer by asking another question, "why because?" The mature ego cannot live with "because," and it does not trust the answer.

Although the steps to manifesting are very straightforward, it is our thoughts that continually get in the way of creating what we desire. One may have years of learning to re-evaluate, sort out, and clean up, before they can manifest effectively on a conscious level. All the thoughts that we grew up with, of being undeserving or unworthy, will have to be dealt with first.

If what you have been doing all your life has not brought you what you truly desire, then is it not about time you tried something new? Is it not self evident that something is not working for you?

Give in to the idea that it can happen for you, and never *give up* on the idea. Accept the fact that you will get what you desire and surrender to the idea that it is already yours. Then get out of the way and let it happen. Believe what you know to be true, that you are the power and you will find a way to make it happen. Know that the choices are coming your way, and you will make the best choice. Do not question the system and you do not even need to know how it works. Just *know* that it does.

Organized religion has done a marvellous job of convincing us that we are "undeserving," and "unworthy." We need to get over that, and we need to move to a different place. These are two concepts that are in our minds only, and have no fact in spirit. They are obstacles to manifesting what we desire, and they are closed doors.

After almost 30 years of not attending a church service, I agreed to go to Vicky's church one Sunday morning. She said it was very upbeat and progressive—I was looking forward to something different, and liberating.

As the speaker moved to the front of the church he raised his arms and started the opening prayer with "Lord, we are so unworthy." My heart felt sick, as did my stomach; my attention faded away like bad breath into the wind. I felt so insulted and angered.

Humanity will find its power once again, when it gives up old thoughts about who is in control of it. The first step is a willingness to let go, to surrender, to accept new thoughts, and to get out of the box. Religion must give up some of its power and return it to its congregation if it hopes to survive.

Mankind must find a willingness to move on, to let go of old outdated beliefs no matter how long we have believed in them, and no matter how well we believe they have served us. Willingness and freedom to accept new philosophies and truths brings with it new experiences, new pleasures and rewards. We can have anything we desire— anything, so long as it is purposeful to our spiritual (personal) desires, and we are committed to getting it.

Imagination

Our emotions follow our thoughts and our imagination, not the other way around, as is the popular belief. Thought is always the first step in manifestation.

The proper use of imagination can drive ideas in the direction we most desire. By using the imagination creatively we can neutralize the negative thoughts or ideas that we now harbour, and open the door for effective manifesting. The imagination is creative. Creativity is natural to each of us and it is what we do best—it is our whole purpose for being in the physical world. Our imagination fosters creativity and our thoughts are always creative.

Use it now, on a conscious level, to rid yourself of the feelings of lack in your life. Pretend that you are rich and that you have lots of money. Picture yourself spending your wealth. Picture your beautiful home, surrounded by the things you desire most. Imagine traveling all over the world with no thoughts about how to pay for it. Use your imagination, and let it work for you.

You are creating a thought pattern that, when dwelled upon long enough, will intensify and manifest into exactly what you imagine. Eventually, any feelings of lack or doubt will be replaced by your new imagined life. Take time each day and quickly go over the new ideas you have about yourself and your life.

Think positively; think successful no matter how hard your ego tries to tell you otherwise. No matter how often the negative feelings keep leaching into your mind, replace them with the thoughts of your abundance. Surround yourself with pictures of what your new life will look like. See yourself in each of those pictures, and simply believe that it is happening. Declare it to the people of the world, and let everybody know what it is you desire, and they will help you manifest it. There is nothing else you have to do. Be true to the new ideas that are going to work for you, as you have been to the old ideas that have not, or no longer work for you. Use your imagination to tell yourself what a wonderful, unique and deserving person you are. Keep repeating these thoughts for as long as it takes, until finally they become your new thought, your only reality. You have a marvellous imagination and it can work for you, it is powerful. You think, you imagine and you create. You will always experience whatever you think or imagine, at some level of your consciousness.

> *"If thou wouldst conquer thy weakness thou must not gratify it."*[23]

This is an easy exercise that is powerful, effective and beneficial. If it does not work for you it is because you do not believe it will, or you have given up before the effect has had a chance to work.

I have been using this exercise for a long time now, and I know that it works for me. I have been chiselling away at my negative thoughts relentlessly for years. I can say, without reservation, that it works for me. It may take some

---

[23] William Penn

time, depending on how rooted your old thoughts are, but it does work. Keep repeating the exercise any time you become aware of negative feelings entering your thoughts.

Repeat to yourself as often as necessary, "*I am worthy, I am intelligent, I am deserving, I can have anything that I desire and no one can stop me, no one!*"

Know This "Great Secret"

Recently Vicky and I, along with two of our circle members, attended a "be a millionaire" seminar. I have entertained the idea of being a millionaire many times in my life. I promised I would donate some of my millions to charity, or help other people, if only I could have it. This is a noble thought, and is self designed to make my ego feel more worthy. However it is laced with feelings of guilt, and of being undeserving, and a failure.

In the last few years, I have lowered my expectations to accommodate the feeling of lack in my life. I have settled for wanting just enough money to live comfortably and not worry about paying the bills. I was willing to settle for less so that I would have enough.

During the seminar I felt pressured into believing I had to want millions of dollars. The speaker pressured me and those that came with me pressured me. I believed I wanted some money, but not millions. I told myself I would just give most of it away and keep just enough to be comfortable. I believed I did not want the responsibility of having that much money. I felt resentful and angry that the people around me were telling me I must have a "millionaire" mind. I did not have to go to this seminar to find this out. I learned from this event that I had just enough, which I already knew—I just didn't realize to what extent I knew it.

I do not have millions of dollars, and the reasons why I do not have millions of dollars are because of the reasons why I "want" millions of dollars.

Vicky has been bugging me with this question ever since the seminar. I kept telling her over again the reasons why I want millions of dollars. Every time she asks me that question, I felt myself getting angrier with her. I feet that she was not listening to me, or perhaps I was just too dense.

It finally dawned on me—the meaning of everything that she has been telling me. Guardian Angels know these things—bless her!

The purpose of desiring millions of dollars is to spend it, and that is the purpose of money. Money has no intrinsic value other than to spend it. Vicky has always had lots of money, because she likes to spend it. Harvey has always had lots of money, because he likes to spend it. Money is worthless until you spend it. We do not need to have a lofty or noble reason for desiring a million dollars. Manifest with purpose, create the million dollars, and then spend it. Then manifest some more for the same purpose. The real reason for having money is not to pay bills, or to be comfortable, happy, or donate it. The real reason is to spend it! Be generous with yourself and manifest millions.

It takes the same thought process to manifest one dollar as it does a million. If you are afraid to ask for more because you think you are undeserving, then that is what you will get back—nothing or less, because you believe you are undeserving. Manifest with authority and know it is you who is doing the creating or manifesting, and be generous. I have now changed my mind about why I desire millions of dollars so that I can spend it.

If knowing you can have millions of dollars or anything else you desire scares you, you may find some comfort in knowing that you will scare the hell out of those who already have it and are not willing to share. Once wealth is distributed evenly, it will level the playing field. Once equity exists amongst us, the major reason for war will be eliminated. War is born from a fear of lack.

Have Purpose with Gratitude

Jerry flew off the roof of his house, "because" it was purposeful. He did not do it to be injured, or to have his parents angry with him. He did not do it because he was an aircraft designer, or because he was stupid. He did it because he was a pilot and pilots fly. I suspect poor quality aircraft design and inexperience were the only reasons he did not fly as far as he wanted. Do not overlook the fact that he did fly. He experienced exactly what he desired, and crash landings are something that all pilots face every time they go up. You must be a pilot before you can crash land.

Make it clear in your mind that you are not asking for something, wishing for something, or hoping to have something. Know that you have the thing or circumstance now, not in the future, but now. Otherwise that is when you will experience getting it, in the future, and you will never experience it now.

Gratitude may be the most important element in manifesting, for it recognizes that you already have what you desire. If you are grateful for your success then you must "already" be successful. If you are grateful for your happiness then you must "already" be happy. It is not something that is going to happen in the future, it is happening now.

Think "gratitude" when you are manifesting, it helps you focus. For example, say to yourself, "I am grateful for my continuing success. I am grateful for the ongoing joy that I am experiencing. I am grateful for the abundance that is mine," and then know that more will follow.

In Conclusion

Manifesting works and we all know it works because it is observable. We see it in our lives everyday. We recreate ourselves every morning when we arise and continue to create throughout the entire day until we fall to sleep again.

I know that we can raise the level of our manifesting to a conscious level; to a level that we can manifest on demand and instantly. There are those around us that do it very well—it is demonstrated and documented.

The ability to manifest consciously on demand, at a higher level, depends directly on the strength of your thought that you can do it. The universal law is non-personal and must be obeyed. The law does not care who is doing the manifesting or what is being manifested or why. It only knows that it has to create what is being commanded of it through the thought process.

There are no persons that are more, or less, deserving to manifest wealth, happiness or joy in their lives. It is those that know how to use the system effectively that manifests a perceived better quality lifestyle. Know that you can have, or do, anything—not because you deserve it, but simply because you desire it.

The system works—you must know that. We all have thoughts hidden away in our minds that say we cannot do this, we are non-deserving or we simply do not believe it. The journey of a thousand steps begins with the first one. Know what it is that you desire. Know its purpose and be honest with yourself. Be relentless in your pursuit of it. Take time out several times each day to include the simple exercise in your daily life to clear your mind of negative thoughts. Look at your life now and know that you created everything in it, and all the events of your life. Clean house (your mind) of the thoughts that do not serve you any longer. Always be generous with yourself. Become a believer and simply manifest, manifest, manifest!

If you accept responsibility for your life and its circumstances, then you also accept the power to change it.

BOOK FOUR

GETTING REAL

PREFACE

The essence of this book lies within the paradigm of my own truth. It is my belief that we, as human beings, control the power of the universe through our thoughts. The purer the thought, the better we are able to influence the forces. Thought is the trigger or switch that moves power. Nothing can move or manifest until there is a thought behind it.

For that reason, we are at the mercy of our own undisciplined random thoughts. Of the more than 65,000 thoughts that run through our heads in one day, only 15% of them focus on what we are engaged in, at the moment. The other 85% are random thoughts about old business.

For the most part, we do not fully manifest what we desire simply because we do not believe that we can. If we have not experienced or witnessed a thing in physical reality, then we have doubts about being able to manifest it. If we have never seen a person jump off a building and fly, we do not believe it is possible. Our thoughts of not being able to do a thing interfere with our ability to do it. It is the doubts that create failure. We create failure because we believe that we will fail.

In truth, it is possible to jump off a building safely. It is also possible to jump off a building and land safely. It is, in fact, possible to jump off a building and fly safely to the ground, 50 stories below.

Re-read the last paragraph. I said, "we do not believe that we can jump off a building and fly." I purposefully left out all the details of the event, leaving you with your imagination and thoughts about how it was not possible. Your immediate thoughts may not focus on how one could actually do it, but why one could not.

You may have envisioned someone jumping from a building, hitting the ground several storeys below, and dying. Everything immediately suggested that the action would not be successful.

In truth, anyone can jump off a building and fly. It is also a fact that most will hit the ground hard and die. The physiology of man does not lend itself well to flying. Nevertheless if one jumps, one does fly.

From our experiences, and those of others, we assume that jumping off a building, and flying successfully without any aids, is not possible. Because we accept that mindset, it becomes part of our truth. No one will ever be able to jump off a roof that is 50 stories high, without safety equipment, and land safe and sound.

Our mindset focuses not on flying, but on hitting the ground and dying. We assume that we will fall rather than rise. We fall because we are heavier than air, and gravity pulls us to the ground. This is a natural law of nature and has always been so. We fix our thoughts on the one law concerning gravity, and have ruled out any other possibilities.

Humanity does not have wings to glide, but it does not necessarily follow that we cannot fly because of that lack. It is obvious that humanity is not equipped to fly successfully, so man must look to other possibilities. Man may not have wings, but it is possible that man can fly by making himself lighter than air, thus overcoming the laws of gravity.

A 250-pound man can make himself lighter by loosing 100 pounds, but he will still be heavier than air, and fall. We know that from experience, anything heavy always falls down.

At one time we held as truth that we would always fall off the edge of the earth if we sailed too far. Then we come up with the thought that the world may be round, and we set out to demonstrate that thought. So maybe it is simply that we need another thought about flying, and then set out to demonstrate that thought.

Matter is the densest form of light, and matter vibrates at the lowest frequency of light. Light is physical yet it can be lighter than air by changing its frequency and density. Because we are light, we have the same attributes as light. We can raise our vibrational level by using thought. It is thought that controls the power to create, and the power is accessible to all. Thought is the key, the switch that closes the path for energy to flow.

Eliminate the notion that you cannot fly, open the door for other possibilities, and you will discover a way to do it. If you believe that a possibility exists, you will eventually find it. If you want to fly without help, make yourself lighter than air, transform yourself. History has shown that it is possible. Raise yourself up, and you can walk on water. As you begin to transform, you raise yourself up, becoming lighter than air. It is not really that far-fetched. History has documented many people who have risen. If you think it is an unfair comparison, then you know why man is not doing it. Because he believes, he cannot. Is this ability reserved for only a few chosen ones? I think not!

A SPIRITUAL MAKEOVER

You may have reached a point in your life that has brought you a new realization to you. Your life sucks, you have missed something along the way, and you now believe there has to be something more. You are off your chosen path and have moved in a direction that is not working for you. Life is a struggle and everyone in it is out for themselves. You want out, you are mad as hell and you do not want anything to do with life anymore. You think to yourself, "take me now."

Is this your new belief, your new reality, your new truth? Has life taught you that it sucks big time. So now you have given up on it. If there ever was a meaning to your life you have forgotten, and you want out.

The good news is that you can get out anytime you want. The bad news is that there is nowhere to go. Heaven and hell are manifestations of your mind—they are not places. There is only one place to go, and that is back to the point where you left off. Life and death are the same thing, they exist in a cycle and like all cycles, the end is the beginning and the beginning is the end.

There is no real escape, you cannot run, and you cannot hide. However, you can use the illusion, or work within it, to hide. You have the key, you are the switch and you can use the unlimited power of the universe to tailor a life that is uniquely yours. You can use your mind to create the life you want, and create all the things you desire. You can do it if you believe you can. You must believe in the possibilities to do so, and you will find the way.

You can fly, but first you must know you can. The possibility must be alive in your mind for it to happen.

Begin now to create the life you desire. Unbelievably, that is exactly what you have been doing all along. You created the life you now have; no one else did it for you, and you created it through choices you made from birth. There is no one to point a finger at, and no one to blame except you. It was your thoughts that got you to this point. If there is no escape from life, and if this life is not the one you want to experience, then you leave yourself only one other choice, "create a new one." You can start from scratch, and use what you now know to come up with something even better, something new and outrageous.

Create your new life from the perspective of knowing you can have anything you desire. Know that you create by making choices from the things that already are. All probabilities of your life already exist. Time and space is the illusion; the past, present and future exist at the same time and in the same place. Know that you exist in the physical world as an illusion, or a projection, and that you have the power over your own life because your life is just a thought—yours! Your life never ends and you do not have to wait for something to happen—you make it happen.

Keep the possibility or choice alive, and create your new life by knowing exactly what it is that you want to experience. Make the conscious choices that will best facilitate the life you so desire.

Your world, the people and circumstances, are figments of your imagination. You bring all of them together into your life so that you may experience the life you are imagining.

If you believe the world is a terrible place, you will bring the people and circumstances into your experience that will reflect that belief. If you believe the world is a beautiful place, you will bring the right people and circumstances into your life that will facilitate that thought. You must always be careful of your thoughts, how and what you think will become your new reality. Be careful what you think, and what you say. You are your

best   friend   and   your   worst   enemy,   and
uncontrolled thoughts and words make it so.

   Make friends with all parts of your existence.
You are a three part being—mind, body and
spirit—this is your true nature, you are a spiritual
being. They are the only things that are real, and
together all parts create in harmony what you
want to experience. If you fall out of harmony with
any aspect of yourself, you will get different results
from your manifesting than what you may have
desired. Because you focus in the physical world,
you must train yourself to commune with the non-
physical spirit through meditation, affirmations,
symbolism, or any other way that facilitates
communication between all the parts.

   There is one very important aspect of your
existence that you will come to realize. You are the
only one here! There is only one soul shared
between all of its individualized parts, and all
parts work in harmony to experience the whole.
All parts must work in agreement with each other,
and there are no innocent victims

   Your mind is part of the collective mind. When
you create the circumstances of your life, others
work with you to make it so. While you may
believe you are alone and separate from the
others, it cannot be this way and you are one with
all others. You are as the finger on your body, you
are called finger, but you are intimately connected
to the rest of the body.

   You cannot kill another body without the
permission of the soul that is working in that
body, just as you would not be able to clap your

hands together without the co-operation of both hands. All aspects of the "one mind" work together, to create the experiences of the individualized mind because, in fact, there is really only one mind.

Keep this in mind as you begin to create your new life's experience. You cannot do anything to others without their consent at some level of consciousness. All others come into your life at your request, to facilitate a thought that you have.

It is you that is doing the giving and taking, because there is only you. When you make choices, you must do so selfishly, because there is no other way to do it. As you choose what you desire, know that it is you who is creating and giving to yourself. If you give to another, you are giving to "another self." If you try to take away from another self, you are taking away "you," from "yourself," leaving only "self."

I have already demonstrated that you cannot take away from "any-self," because there is only "yourself." No matter what you take away from *self* or put in front of *self*, there is only *self*. When you take from another *self* you feel a loss, not a gain. The other is there to help you experience "the taking," or they would not be there at that time and place. It is the right hand taking from the left—you are not adding anything.

All of you are simply in existence to experience self; the whole is experiencing self through the individualized pieces of self. You experience your physical world through relationships with others.

Without the others, you cannot define yourself or experience self.

You cannot define yourself as skinny, if there are no others that are fat. You cannot define yourself as tall if there are no others that are short. You cannot define yourself as good, if there are no others that are bad. You create your opposite to give meaning and purpose to your present physical experience, and you are not at the mercy of circumstances—you are creating them.

SEVEN PLACES TO START

The seven steps I am proposing below are guides. You do not have to follow them. In fact, it works in your best interest to create your own unique steps for a new life, based on your own priorities. The seven steps I have created will open your mind to other possibilities, and you can use them as a guide.

I do not advocate changing anything in your life that is working for you. What I propose for you to do is eliminate all the things that are not working. What I am suggesting is that you be perfectly selfish in establishing a framework, one that will guide you in the direction you have chosen. Use these steps to create a new life, a life that is uniquely yours—not the result of pressure from other people that would mould you to their image.

As you begin to change your life, people will not understand you. Most of them will not even want to know what is happening to you. Those closest to you will try to change you back to the way you were. Those people are currently in your life that cannot accept the changes will gradually disappear from it. Others that are attracted to your style will replace those people. The right people will start appearing from out of nowhere, you will not have to look for them. All these people will be the symbols of your new philosophy and belief system. Study them, and accept the gifts they bring you. Their gift is awareness, your awareness, and they are a mirrored image of it.

The fact that you have come this far is evidence enough for me that your mind is already open, and that you are starting to look outside of your box. You were never wrong where you were, and you will never be right where you are going. You will simply begin to know what works, and what does not work for you. Every step along the way is appropriate for you, considering the model you have of the world and how you see yourself in relation to it. It appears that you are now ready to be pro-active in your own life.

Realize always that you are in this world, you are creating it, but you are not of it. Do not think little—be grand about your thoughts. These lifetimes that you are experiencing are just short sleepovers. You are much bigger than this world or the universe. You are all that is, there is nothing else. Create your life in that thought, and do not give your power away again. You must grow to take responsibility for your life. Accept the circumstances of your life as your creation, and you will always retain the power to change it.

There is no one out there who is going to help you. If you are sick, it is because, at some level of consciousness, it is what you want. If you are struggling it is because, at some level, you want to experience it. If you have an accident, it was by your design. If you are wealthy, joyful and live in abundance, that is also because it is what you wanted in your life. The only reason, ONLY REASON you cannot have anything you desire is that you *think* you cannot.

There is no prerequisite for spirituality—you are spiritual by nature, it is who you are. There is no payment or penance to get what you desire, unless you think there is. There are no courses, no rituals or ceremonies to attend, to become spiritual. It has nothing to do with intellect or deserving and there is no guru, priest or holy man that can give it to you. There is quit simply, nothing to give. You are the physical embodiment of all that is. You arc the key, the switch or activator, to the power that creates.

When are you going to start to change things? If not now, when? If not you, who? Whose life is it? Who is doing the driving?

RELIGION

Religion is man's attempt to explain spirituality. There is nothing right or wrong with religion, in as much as there is nothing in spirit that is "right or wrong." There is only that which works, and that which does not work, in experiencing what it is that you desire.

Religion is an attempt to explain who you are and why you are here—it is man's attempt. It is man that created religion and it is man that created the doctrine of religion and for the sake of argument I mean man—not woman.

All religions are valid because all that humanity creates is legitimate. They are physical manifestations of the thoughts of those that believe and are demonstrated physically in the symbols of the religion. God does not need religion, and has no thoughts about it one way or the other. God creates through humanity all that he thinks.

It is man who wrote the stories written about in the holy writings of religion. For the one or the thousands of people that follow a religion, they leave a signpost that physically demonstrates their spiritual awareness and their relationship to others, and their environment.

Religion is a museum that expresses in a "." of time, a thought process. It is an end of a thought process, what you put at the conclusion of the sentence. The thoughts are formed first, then the statue is built, and it goes nowhere.

Religion is not absolute truth. It is the believer's truth, created by them. Truth is as liquid as the water that surrounds the earth. All truth becomes a remnant of a person or society that believed in it at one time.

All established religious doctrine is not truth. It is death and non-life because its truth does not change. Doctrine attempts to explain the truth and keep it static. Truth is about change and growth. Life cannot exist in the realm of religious doctrine unless it changes.

Use religion to motivate you past what it teaches. Use it as you would any historical belief system, as a step leading to another. Do not allow yourself to become boxed. Chew away at the corners until you can see the light, and then leave it behind. Take the best of it and add it to something new. Think about it. How can you apply what you have learned from religion to make it work in your present life? Any religion or belief system should be a stepping stone, not an end unto itself.

The true test of any religious doctrine must be demonstrated physically. You live in a physical world, and this is where the religion must be focused. This is where you need the guidance, and where it is going, to do the most good. If your religion promises you eternal love, peace, and abundance in this world, you should be able to see the physical results. You cannot live on promises. A promise is something that always happens in the future, therefore religion can promise you nothing because what they promise is never manifested. Your belief system must be grounded where you need it the most. Enlightenment will lead you to the "promised" land and it will be because you have created it now, not because you have suffered through a lifetime to get it.

You will not have what you desire through faith, hope, belief or promise. You will have what you desire when you decide to create it. Hope, faith and belief are ways to lead you to knowing, but they never get you there. You will have what you desire when you leave hope, faith, and belief, and move on to knowing. You can have what you desire when you know you already have it and this is the fastest route.

Create, create, create, that is your purpose. Create your religions and faiths around what you believe today, then move on and create another.

Leave the trail for others to follow, but do not get hung up with the creation. The creation will die, as all things do.

The power in your life comes from knowing that you have it. Do not give it up for a measure of security, and promise from religious leaders. They cannot take care of your soul—it does not belong to them. They cannot promise you heaven or hell, and they cannot promise you what they do not have themselves. Enlightenment comes when you are ready to receive it. No one can give it to you. You will not find your truth in religious texts or doctrine. You always create truth, and then recreate it when it no longer fits into your beliefs.

You cannot make someone else's truth yours. You can adapt, add, take away and expand, but you will simply have created something new. Truth belongs to no man, because it changes all the time. What you grasp onto disappears in the wink of an eye. What you have reached for is not there by the time your hand has moved into position, because truth is alive and it moves.

The small businessperson with a single store does not declare himself successful in creating a franchise. The franchise is successful only when it is sold and there are trails of stores to follow. Continued growth is the success of a franchiser. When the growth stops, the business eventually dies.

A wise man would never run to the highest mountaintop and yell out that he has found God, because he would know that it is "he," that was never lost and there is no one to tell.

Is it the whole that is trying to find the pieces, or is it the pieces that are trying to find the whole, and does it really matter? The salvation of your soul is just not necessary because it does not need to be salvaged; it is never lost or damaged.

If it is humanity's desire to experience ugliness, humankind will create a world that allows him to experience it. He will gather other souls that will allow him to create what he desires. If a man wants to experience war, he will create a world that allows him to facilitate the experience of war.

The so-called "innocent victims," are actually volunteers (souls) that have agreed to be in the right place and the right time to allow such carnage to manifest. All souls agree at some level of consciousness, otherwise it could not happen.

Holy wars are full of such willing victims. You do not have to look far to know that. No event can happen without the willingness of another soul at some level to participate. Your right hand cannot slap you in the face, unless your face agrees to it.

Religion does not teach you any of these things. Religion has its own agenda and survives on the fear of your soul being lost. Religion clearly demonstrates its inability to grow and move on. Where there is no growth, there is no life.

Religion is not about life. It is about a promise of an afterlife, and a manifestation of humanity's fear of the awesome power that it represents. It is an outward sign of our immaturity, and our position along the evolutionary path.

Yes, I am for religion. It brings awareness into our lives. All religions and faith systems are relevant and purposeful. They are stepping-stones or sign posts. They are outward manifestations of how the believers are thinking at the time. They are physical symbols that only beings living in a physical world can relate to, and they are appropriate.

RELATIONSHIPS

All relationships are about you, not the other. Because you are always in relationship with self—your-self!

Personal relationships are the hardest to maintain, and they are the most meaningful. Relationships are gifts from strangers: they offer the best opportunity for expressing who and what you are.

The very word "relationship" gives you a hint as to why they occur. In the physical relative world, you define yourself always in relationships. You are in relationship to everything that is physical and is not.

The creator himself is shapeless and formless energy. He cannot define Himself because He is everything that is. There is nothing else for Him to compare Himself to, in relationship to himself. In order to give definition to self, God the creator, creates definition through its individualized pieces of itself—"souls," and this is what you are. You are an individualized piece of the creator experiencing everything that the creator is and is not, thus giving the creator the opportunity to define self.

You give the creator the opportunity to look back at self and observe that it is either this or that. It is natural for all living things to define themselves, to know who and what they are.

The creator formed relativity, or time and space, for this to happen. Everything is relative in time and space. Everything in the universe is relative to something and nothing at all.

As the creator moves to define Himself so does his individual parts. What you are doing here, in this lifetime, is simply deciding who you are through all the experiences of your life. There is no other purpose to your life than self-actualization, definition and experience.

Close, personal, intimate relationships give you the perfect opportunity to express or demonstrate who you are. No matter who defines the relationship, we do it in two different ways—yours and your partners—and the partners will not define it exactly the same way.

You draw to yourself the person who is best suited to allow you the opportunity to experience yourself as you imagined, whether it is a one-night stand or a monogamous lifetime relationship.

Falling in love may be one of the weakest reasons for entering into a long term relationship, unless it is simply to experience physical love. Physical love ends very quickly and turns into something else. You may be left with nothing to hold the relationship together.

The one who is closest to you should be the one that challenges you the most. It will take lots of love, and patience to maintain the relationship, but the rewards are huge.

In a relationship entered into for the purpose of personal growth, it is always a win/win situation. You always come out of it with a realization of growth and maturity, and never a loss.

If you consciously go into a relationship for growth, you will always find it. When the growth stops, you will know it and be able to make adjustments, or end it. Because of your higher awareness, both of you will come away with growth, which is what you went into it for. If you happen to fall in love, consider that a bonus. You will not move away from the relationship hating each other, where there is true growth.

The best reason to be together is that you want to be, and not that you need each other. Co-dependency does not foster personal growth, but limits it.

Relationships with family, friends, co-workers and others, will all bring more opportunities for personal growth.

In relationships, notice that there is always one amongst them who irritates you the most. That one brings the greatest gift and you come face to face with the one who represents a part of you that you have buried, a part you do not like and have rejected. Treat this person with the greatest respect, and welcome them. Give patience to this one and observe what it is about this person that you do not like, and you will gain insight into what aspect of yourself you do not like. It is actually an opportunity given to you for change and self-improvement.

Be selfish about who you bring into your life. You do not have to maintain relationships that do not add to growth, whether they are personal, family or friends. Guilt or obligation is a denial of self, and should not be a reason for maintaining any kind of relationship, unless guilt or obligation is what you wish to experience. Always consider how you see yourself and where you are going. Attract relationships that enhance your life, that challenge you, and inspire you to become greater than you already are.

POLITICS

As with relationships, one must be ruthless in choosing a party or leader that represents one's best interests. Politics is an altruistic relationship, with a party or leader that manifests itself physically. Politics and political leaders are an outward manifestation of a spiritual belief system. Laws are formed, and passed around the current belief system of the electorate.

A voter chooses a political party or leader because the choice represents the thought process of the voter.

You may choose a socialist party because you feel that the cumulative wealth should be controlled and distributed by government. You may choose a conservative party because it represents old values and is basically slow to change. A return to established values may suit members of this party.

It is the responsibility of an empowered government to represent the wishes and established moral values of the people they represent. The government uses moral principles to establish laws that represent the values of its constituents in time and place.

Highly enlightened people need less government because they always do things that are life-affirming, and because they understand, at a higher level, the connection between all living things.

What is in the best interest of another, is in the best interest of each individual, because in truth we are all one. It is just good politics to "do unto another as you would yourself." Serving another, in short, is serving self. It is the most selfish and worthy moral ethic. Because we are creating leaders and parties that represent our own values, they already reflect physically what our thought process is.

Dictators, kings and presidents are not in power by accident. They are created by a majority at a subconscious level, to represent the majority and pass laws that are in harmony with popular thought at any one time or place. Political leaders do for us what we believe we cannot do for ourselves.

Voting is a major demonstration of internal dialogue, and one should be selfish in that the new leader or party reflects your thoughts about your environment, and the people with which you share it.

Giving way to what others wish is denial of yourself, and how you would model your world. You cannot vote for another but for yourself. Your leader is 'you,' presenting yourself before your fellow man, and declaring how it is going to be. He is your voice ringing out your values and making them public.

Politics is spirituality in motion, manifesting laws that reflect your thought process.

CAREER

Your job is one of the most important aspects of your physical life. Because you spend most of your waking hours, working to support yourself, your job is a significant factor in your life. It would follow then that your job, and the people associated with it, will have a major impact on your life.

Statistically, most people are in jobs that are not suited to them. In North America, you will have a career change at least five times in your life. Most people do not like the job they are working in. This is evidenced in the increased numbers of new small businesses and bankruptcies. In a study, researchers found that most employees would take a small cut in their wages, for the opportunity to have a say in how the business is operated. Most people want to have some control over their lives, but feel helpless or ignored in the job process.

Many of you do not know what you want to do when you leave school, and you have not thought about a career. You have skills and assets that are yours but you are not trained to equate skills with careers. The only thing you know is that you need a job.

Other times there are no jobs available that suit your skills, and you take what you can get.

Desperation is a poor prerequisite for a job application, and a meaningful career.

It is important to choose wisely, the job that you will have. However, it is not the end, and choosing a poor quality job that does not suit you can be a step in the right direction. If you are determined to get into something in harmony with your skills, the job will give you some cash, or means to move onto something else.

The danger here is that you settle in, and become comfortable with your income and start spending it. You lose site of what it is you really want—that is to be happy and secure on your terms. Having money in your pocket brings more opportunity to make poor choices. As you look over your neighbour's fence, and notice the toys that he has, you begin to want.

You start to imagine what it would be like to have it all, and your thoughts are turned away from what you really want. Freedom and happiness give way to keeping up with the Joneses. You set a trap for yourself. You find a way not to take responsibility for the effort it takes to move out, and find the career you have always wanted.

You will most likely spend your money keeping up to the image that is expected of you by your peers and community. From here, you get into a permanent relationship, and acquire more responsibility. After you have spent your money, you go into debt for loans and mortgages.

You have become successful at fitting into the status quo. The trap has been sprung and you are the catch. You took the easy way out which, in fact, turned into the hardest way out. Now with all the responsibility, you have the perfect excuse for not moving forward. You have become the one you despise and condemn.

You are now blinded to any way out, and you hate your job and the people in it. There is constant pressure on you to stay with the job because of guilt and obligations. You may turn to alcohol, drugs, television or other diversions to numb your existence. This affects your relationship with your family, and you may become impatient and abusive. Many of you will hate your life and the circumstances of it, or even worse, you settle for it. At least with hate, it may motivate you to do something about it.

Hard choices await you, and you are going to have to find the determination and the means to break free. You are going to have to convince your family and friends of your new intentions, and get their cooperation and support to move away from what you have, or you are going to have to leave them and separate.

These possibilities are threatening, and overwhelming to most. Breaking free is the hardest thing you will ever do in your life. It takes tremendous energy and resolve to do it. It will be the most painful thing you can do to yourself, and the people in your life.

The truth is that the love for self must be greater than the love of others. You cannot give love if you have no love for self. You have become a provider, and maybe a very good one—inside you may be dead. Families are great for support but they have their own agenda, and will fight to keep your support. If you are very lucky and have nurtured them spiritually over the years, they may stick with you and support your change.

This is a hard way to be educated: and once you have moved away from your path, it takes more energy to move back to it. You create all the circumstances of your life through the choices you make. Poor choices come from poor thought. You are not the victim of circumstances, you create them. Take the responsibility for them and you will have the power to change them. You must own a thing before you can give it away. If you do not own a thing then you have less or no power over it.

Awareness brings determination, and if you believe you do not have choices, than you also must believe that you do not have power to make any.

The real power in your life comes from choosing wisely, what you want in the first place. Once a choice is made, it expresses the power that you own, and it is absolute and final. From there you are automatically determined to bring that choice into manifestation. Choices will automatically come your way that will lead you to the place you want to be. You do not have to look for them; they will be there if only you recognize them. You do not have to control the situation, but simply make a choice. The choice is the switch, the trigger that brings what you desire to you. You are the master, and you do not have to find—it finds you.

Seek and you "shall not" find. Choose and it is already yours. The real joy in your life comes from the love you feel for yourself. That love is expressed in the love that you pass onto others.

In your career, choose wisely, and do not be in a hurry. Plant the seed, embrace the tree, and you will feel the weight of your patience at fruition.

HOME

Home is where the heart is, and of all the physical things in your life, your home expresses who you are. Your house, and the objects in it are symbols of your thought process. One can know oneself quickly and accurately by associating these symbols. The lack of symbols in your home is just as revealing. Your home is personal and it is a landmark, a signpost that says this is who I am and where I am now, in this moment.

Your home is a museum or an encyclopaedia of your life. It is ground zero, an anchor for you. When I look up from my keyboard I see pictures and objects that remind me of who I am, and what I am thinking in this time and place. Every object contains a memory. The memory is in the object itself and infrequently in my mind.

The objects should reflect a life, not a corpse. A home can become a morgue if life has stopped moving. A home should no more remain static than your own life. Keep your home up, redecorate, paint, move things around, bring things in, and take things out. Express yourself physically in your home, in balance with what you are thinking in this time and place. Move old objects into a special place you can visit from time to time, but do not cling to them. Your better days are experienced now if you are growing—and they are not the good old days.

It is also important to live where there is the most energy. Find areas where there is a lot of growth, both human and plant life. Some areas in the world have greater energy than others. These are energy vortexes. There are several known areas in the world where the energy is the strongest. For example, the west coast of North America is one of these vortexes.

Keep many living things in and around your home. Animals especially, bring a lot of energy into your life. Pets are extremely important. The love of a pet can enrich your life tremendously.

Read books on Feng Shui, incorporate some of these concepts into your life. As you begin to add these things into your home, you begin to give greater dimension to yourself.

Your home is your temple, keep it as such—it is your sanctuary. Have a quite place and time in your home, where you and your family can meditate and commune with quality learning, and the exchange of ideas.

Remove poor quality low energy objects from your home, and try to use as many natural products as possible. Add lots of fresh air to your home and use only natural scents. Keep your ventilation system clean of human waste, dust mites and bacteria.

Consider all the things in your home that affect your natural health and breathing. Put value on your health, and spend what ever it takes to keep it clean and dust free.

Do what ever it takes to feel comfortable in your home. If you really want to know how you are thinking and feeling deep down inside, look at your home. Whether your home is as sterile as a hospital, or as dirty as a pigpen, it is a symbol of your deeper thoughts. Either extreme is unhealthy.

Balance all things in your home, including its furnishings, plant life, its colours, the air, the sunlight and the cleanliness. Balance silence with music. Beware of the energy levels of the sounds that you use. Some music is very negative and drains your energy. Mix the sounds of laughter with the gentle whimpers of crying, sighs and involuntary moans and groans of sex. Express yourself in sound, always. Play an instrument, or bring in musical friends to entertain you and your guest. Party it up a bit, have friends and guests in frequently for dinner. Eating in a group has great potential for receiving energy.

Bring fresh food into your home for preparation. Do not eliminate prepared food—remember that balance is the key word. Sometimes it is best just to eat junk food occasionally, than to increase stress levels by taking time to cook. Again balance your food and the time needed to prepare it.

There is no place like home, and everyone has both fond and disturbing memories of home. What ever your experience was when you were younger, you now have a choice as a free-spirited adult. Create your environment and manifest comfort, security, health, love and freedom in your home.

Beware of falling into the trap of believing that you have to spend lots of money, and go into debt, to create your home. If you choose this route, you will move away from something that is very positive, to something that is very negative. Even if you can afford the payments now, you may not be able to later. Plant the seeds and have patience. Once you have made the choice, the opportunity will come your way. Your choice will bear fruit; it is the law of the universe. Be realistic and do not try to control the forces.

LEISURE TIME

Of all the things you do, your leisure time says the most about you. Most of us believe that what we do on our own time is our choice. We also believe we do not have a choice about work, or other responsibilities, and so we give grace to our leisure time.

After five days of work, the last two become sacred to us. For the most part, we put leisure time on hold and we prioritize our lives around work and responsibilities. When the weekend comes, we race into our leisure activities with great gusto and fervour, as though we will never have another opportunity again. Or, we collapse in front of the TV, and remain lifeless until our partner motivates us with guilt and threats.

Amongst other pastimes, I play golf. Golf is the great equalizer of all sports. It is a head game, where one plays against oneself. If you want to see into the thoughts of any one individual, find someone who plays golf.

In golf there is more time to think, as you walk along the fairways, and one tends to react to situations on the course as they would in any other part of their life. In other sports, one reacts physically and quickly, and is not as easily affected by personal baggage. Other more physical sports may act as a release for stress. Golf tends to create more, unless one is in a good frame of mind and not carrying the week's baggage.

Spending leisure time is like spending money. It needs to be managed well, because there is so little of it.

Choose the activities that give you the most pleasure, and under no circumstances get involved in activities that you have been pressured into, or have had guilt trips laid on you by others. If you are reluctant to do these things, you will generate negative energy. If you deny yourself, by giving into something you do not want to do, you commit the greatest blasphemy of all—denial of self.

If you are truly doing it for someone else, because you see yourself as a caring, helpful person, even though you may not want to do it, it is in your best interest to do so. It is an opportunity to demonstrate who you are, a caring, helpful individual. It is an opportunity to reaffirm your finer qualities.

Activities that involve movement and fresh air are beneficial. Fun, happy things work in your best interest. Volunteer activities that others may see as work, are recreational to those that love to give.

Ask one who volunteers a lot, why they do it. Most often, their answer will be because it makes them feel good to contribute. If it makes you feel good first, and it defines you as one who helps or gives and you are not doing it out of guilt, then the time is well spent. View volunteerism as an opportunity to do something positive for yourself first. You will never be disappointed, and volunteering will take on a completely different meaning. Be rationally selfish about it. You are not there to change the world, but because you feel good doing something about changing the world, in this fashion.

Pick activities that fit your personality, and do not take away from time with friends and family. Get involved with the activity because you want to. Leisure time is life—enhancing and affirming, so choose your activities accordingly. It is a great opportunity to enhance the quality of life around you. Of course, there is nothing wrong with lying around on the couch, if you see yourself as a couch potato. You are re-affirming who you are, and you are living your truth.

LIFESTYLE

Your lifestyle is who you are. It is your ego, your personality coming through. Your lifestyle is a physical manifestation of your thought process. It is how you see yourself in relationship to your environment, and it is unique to you.

Your lifestyle is freely yours, it is what you have chosen. At all levels, you choose how you are going to live, and your lifestyle is a physical portrait that says, "I'm here, this is who I am." Because your corporal body is who you are to most people—you will be judged by how you dress, how you act, your sexual orientation, your politics and religion.

Your physical body is an illusion, but it is all anyone has to judge you by, except those that are the closest and most intimate with you. Your body and lifestyle can be camouflaged to cloak what is hiding beneath your skin, and it is therefore not very reliable. No one really knows what the purpose of the individual's soul is—and most of the time, not even the individual.

One's lifestyle is the most elastic and transitory aspect of a physical existence. One can give the appearance of being rich, simply by dressing that way. The same individual can dress poorly, and be judged as poor.

In the realm of illusion of which we all live, illusion is most convincing when the deceiver is also convinced by their deception. Because over 60% of us are visual, we judge on what we see. For many it is all they need to know, to make an evaluation.

A change of lifestyle can be very powerful as an affirmation, when we try to convince ourselves of where we want to be, and under what circumstances we wish to conduct ourselves.

Role models are very powerful in an individual's struggle to emulate a particular lifestyle. Many of us, from time to time during our lifetime will go through an identity crisis as we try to determine our place in this world. By choosing a role model and copying their lifestyle, we can sometimes make believe that we are they. As long as we are not lost in the illusion, we can often change our own lifestyle into the one that we want, simply by copying.

As infants we begin to identify ourselves with those around us; we try to be them. We copy the movements of our parents, brothers and sisters, because we think we are they. As we gain more understanding, we begin to realize we are not them at all. We cannot do the same things, we look different and we do not even like the same things. We start to imitate people we see on TV, and in our community, trying to come up with an identity. Although we have a name, we do not have our own lifestyle. We identify and are identified with our families.

From here on in, for most of our life, we struggle to find our own individuality. We are told by family and friends of our uniqueness, and how it is important to focus on our own talents and qualities, and to be ourselves.

For all of this encouragement, they never take off the tether. We find out it is okay to range out and find out who we are, with the qualification that we do not move too far right or left. It is okay to be an individual, but not different. We can be sexual, but not bisexual or gay. We can be religious, but not protestant or apostolic. We can be political, but not liberal or conservative. It is okay to be ourselves, as long as we do not push any buttons. It is okay to ask questions, but not be critical or ask the wrong questions.

How does one find a lifestyle, and what is it that we have to do to be recognized as an individual with purpose? How do we become real?

We become real by, for the most part, adapting what works, and discarding what does not work in our lives. We take responsibility for our lives, and live with the consequences of pushing buttons and pushing limits. We do not make excuses or lie.

You cannot have any kind of lifestyle that is uniquely yours if you get involved with deception and illusion. Lying denies who you are, and it is the worst blasphemy. If you paint a self-portrait and then declare it is not you, you have fooled only yourself.

If you want to be taken seriously, then you must be honest with yourself and others, and make no excuses for the way you are. If you see yourself as dishonest, then be honest with yourself and live a dishonest life. Your dishonesty comes from acting honest, when you know yourself not to be. You can be honest by being dishonest, but not by pretending to be honest.

No matter how you see yourself, always live up to that image, as long as it is working for you. At some point, you may find that what you are doing no longer works, and you will have to make adjustments. Be honest with yourself, and move to a position that you can live with.

If your life is a continuous struggle, it is only because you are not acting in accord with who you really are, and who you really are is not your body. When you get to the point that you do not want to fight the system any longer, you will find out that you have been fighting yourself. You have been living up to an image that is not really you, and a lifestyle that took you away from yourself. At this point give in, but do not give up.

Despite challenges, obstacles and opposition, a life that is lived wholly is honest. You will never perceive your life as a struggle, but as an adventure, where you set the limits and the conditions—where you lead and not follow. An adventure cannot exist without challenges.

True leaders never stop to look behind for followers. They live their own life and always look forward. They are true to themselves and never apologize. They are honest about whom they are, and what it is they want to accomplish.

An honest person carves out their own lifestyle. It is never too late to declare who you are, and what you want to experience. Your lifestyle, so far, has led you to this moment, and therefore has had purpose. No life is wasted, or is without purpose.

It is not dishonest to change a lifestyle either. In fact, changes in lifestyle are practical and represent movement towards enlightenment and growth. Life does not stay the same—why should you think your life would be any different?

Lifestyle changes are inevitable with awareness and enlightenment. There is life outside of the box, and that may mean you have to change many things about yourself to fully appreciate what your new environment may bring.

Expect several changes in your life, and welcome them as a sign that you are moving forward. When you die, they put you in a box for a good reason. There is no life in the box.

Always choose life, and move away from any box, you find yourself in. When you see the light it is a sign, run to it. It is your time to move to the next level.

Conclusion

It is not hard to imagine that by adopting any of the seven steps I listed in the previous chapters, your life will also change.

That is the secret of building a new life, start by changing something. First, you must make up your mind for change, then slowly methodically do something about it.

You are not God, you are God manifesting in the physical world as an individualized piece of self. Absolute laws of nature govern you while you are in physical form. You must live by those laws. For instance, the law of gravity, the law of cause and effect, or karma.

Retribution and punishment are a manifestation of the physical world. Karmic debt does not exist as indebtedness, but karma may extend into the next physical life if it is not balanced. Karma is the law of cause and effect. Whatever you cause to happen, you can expect to experience its effect eventually. It is man who punishes—not God. The thought of punishment brings into your reality the opportunity to experience it.

You have absolute, unconditional freedom to live your physical life the way that you see fit. You never have, or ever will need, anyone's permission to do so. You are the sole creator of your life's circumstances. All possibilities, or probabilities, exist in the same time and space, and you create by choosing from these probabilities.

If you want to live your life by your rules, you must choose to do so. The next step, following a thought that manifests it into physical reality, is the spoken word. It is the key, or switch, that allows for the flow of energy and creation. That word is "choose." "I choose to live my life..." The word "choose" is absolute, it is final. After spoken, there is only delivery or deed. I choose the red shirt over the blue shirt. The choice of the blue shirt no longer exists in your reality once you choose the red shirt.

In creating a spiritual makeover in your life, you must choose to do so.

Forsaking all others, you choose for yourself first. Once you have made your choice, all things that do not pertain to it will disappear from your life, and all things that are relevant will be drawn to you. It is a natural law that whatever you choose shall be yours. It cannot work any other way, unless you see yourself as powerless, and at that point, you are still manifesting that choice. You give your power to another, and live with the consequences.

Choices are not always made from a conscious level. You must be in tune with your thoughts before you utter the words. You may not always get what you bargain for, if you are not perfectly clear in your thought process.

Change will come when you decide to make it. This is not a promise, it is a guaranty. The only descending factor in this equation is your thought about why it will not work. To that extent shall your creation be made manifest.

ISBN 141207752-4